Up & Running
with Carbon Copy Plus

Up & Running
with Carbon Copy Plus™

Marvin Bryan

San Francisco • Paris • Düsseldorf • Soest

Acquisitions Editor: Dianne King
Series Editor: Joanne Cuthbertson
Editor: Judith Ziajka
Technical Editor: Dave Clark
Production Editor: Carolina Montilla
Word Processor: Deborah Maizels
Book Designer: Elke Hermanowski
Icon Designer: Helen Bruno
Artist: Eleanor Ramos
Screen Graphics: Cuong Le
Desktop Production Artist: Helen Bruno
Proofreader: Hilda van Genderen
Indexer: Ted Laux
Cover Designer: Archer Designs

Screen reproductions produced by XenoFont.

SYBEX acknowledges and thanks Microrim for the use of software and
for the support of its staff.

XenoFont is a trademark of XenoSoft.
SYBEX is a registered trademark of SYBEX, Inc.

Library of Congress Card Number: 90-70870
ISBN: 0-89588-709-6

Manufactured in the United States of America
10 9 8 7 6 5 4 3 2 1

Up & Running

Let's say that you are comfortable with your PC. You know the basic functions of word processing, spreadsheets, and database management. In short, you are a committed and eager PC user who would like to gain familiarity with several popular programs as quickly as possible. The Up & Running series of books from SYBEX has been developed for you.

Who this book is for

This clearly structured guide shows you in 20 steps what the product can do, how you make it work, and how soon you can achieve practical results.

What this book provides

Your Up & Running book thus satisfies two needs: It describes the program's capabilities, and it lets you quickly get acquainted with the program's operation. This provides valuable help for a purchase decision. You also receive a 20-step basic course that provides a solid foundation in the program—even if you're a beginner with scant prior knowledge.

The benefits are plain to see. First, you will invest in software that meets your needs, because, thanks to the appropriate Up & Running book, you will know the program's features and limitations. Second, once you purchase the product, you can skip the instruction manual and learn the basics of the program by following the 20 steps.

We have structured the Up & Running books so that the busy user spends little time studying documentation and the beginner is not burdened with unnecessary text.

Structure of the book

A clock shows your work time for each step. This indicates how much time you can expect to spend on each step with your computer.

Clock

Naturally, you'll need much less time if you only read through the steps rather than carrying them out at your computer. You can also save some time by scanning the short notes in the margins to find the most important sections within a step.

Three symbols are used to highlight points of special note. These symbols and their meanings are shown below:

Symbols

Action

Tip

Warning

An Up & Running book cannot, of course, replace a book or manual containing advanced applications. However, you will get the information needed to put the program to practical use and to learn its basic functions.

The first step covers software in relation to hardware requirements. You'll learn whether the program can operate with
your hardware. Various methods for starting the program are
also explained.

The remaining 19 steps demonstrate basic functions, using
examples or short descriptions. You also learn about various
facilities for printing data, displaying it on the screen, and im-
porting and exporting it. The last steps cover special program
features, such as a built-in macro language, additional editing
facilities, or additional programs provided by third parties. If
information regarding recently announced program versions
is available at printing time, new features are introduced to
the extent possible.

An Up & Running book will save you time and money.

SYBEX is very interested in your reaction to the Up & Running series. Your opinions and suggestions will help all of our
readers, including yourself.

Preface

It's difficult—some say impossible—to be in two places at once. Yet with Carbon Copy Plus, you can almost accomplish this. You can sit at a desk in New York, let's say, and operate a computer on another desk in Los Angeles. You can run programs, create new files and directories, install software, conduct diagnostic tests, and talk back and forth on screen with the person who normally uses that far-distant computer.

Once you perform a set of functions for a computer at one location, you can use your copy of Carbon Copy Plus to call another computer in Chicago or Atlanta or Anchorage and perform the same functions all over again. Carbon Copy Plus offers the perfect way to provide detailed technical support to remote locations that don't have support personnel on site.

Operate a remote computer

If, on the other hand, you're the person at the remote location trying to master some new program or one that doesn't seem to behave, with Carbon Copy Plus you can sit back and watch your monitor as an expert from across town or across the country makes everything right, with no need to see you or your machine.

Receive help from afar

Of course, there are limits to what Carbon Copy Plus can do. If something's wrong with your hardware, Carbon Copy Plus is no substitute for an in-the-flesh person with a screwdriver.

However, for those many, many situations where tweaking the software will correct the problem, it's Carbon Copy Plus to the rescue!

This book will teach you how to install, configure, and use Carbon Copy Plus—whether you're the one who'll be giving help or the one who'll receive it. The 20 easy steps you'll

*Learn
Carbon
Copy Plus
in 20 easy
steps*

find here will, as the title implies, get you up and running with Carbon Copy Plus in a hurry.

Incidentally, this program can also be used for terminal emulation, so you can exchange information from your PC with mainframes or bulletin boards. This book discusses these applications as well.

If you haven't bought Carbon Copy Plus yet, this book provides a quick tour of its features and can help you make your purchasing decision.

—Marvin Bryan

Table of Contents

Step 1

Installing the Master Disk

To use Carbon Copy Plus, you must first install and configure the master program disk to tell the program the hardware you have and the way you'll be using the product. The basic installation and configuration takes only a few minutes, after which you can start working with the software. However, for regular use you'll want to go beyond the basic configuration to customize the program further. Customization details are provided in later steps.

In this first step, you'll learn the hardware and software requirements for Carbon Copy Plus (almost any IBM PC or compatible computer can run Carbon Copy Plus), and you'll walk through the installation of the master disk, which has to be done only once.

Checking Your Hardware and Software

You can run Carbon Copy Plus on any IBM PC, XT, AT, PS/2, or compatible computer with at least 256K memory, one disk drive, an available serial port, and one of the following graphics cards: CGA, EGA, VGA, or Hercules. Two computers communicating with each other through the program don't need to have the same kind of graphics card.

You can connect two computers by wiring them together through a null modem cable connected to a serial port on each machine. In this case, of course, you'll need to have the cable, which can be supplied by almost any computer store or mail-order dealer. Be sure your null modem cable is long enough to reach between the two units.

You can wire computers together

However, most people buy Carbon Copy Plus so that someone at one location can operate a computer at a distant location miles or even thousands of miles away. In this typical situation, each computer must be connected to a modem, either internally (that is, on a card inside the PC) or through a standard serial cable, and each modem must be connected to a telephone line. The modem can be almost any standard Hayes-compatible model.

For either a direct link between two PCs with a null modem cable or communication through a dial-up connection using modems and telephone lines, each computer must be running a separate copy of Carbon Copy Plus, with its own individual serial number.

To use the terminal emulator feature, you'll need only one copy of the program.

PCs must be running DOS 2.0 or or a later version.

Copies of Carbon Copy Plus on 5.25-inch disks are furnished on two 360K floppy disks—the master disk, which displays a serial number, and the utility disk, which is labeled Utility. Copies in the 3.5-inch format combine both the master and utility files on a single 720K disk.

If you'll be running the program on a floppy disk system, you'll need one or two blank, formatted disks available to make a working copy. If you'll be copying the program to a hard disk, the extra disks are not essential.

Preparing the Master Disk

Once you've prepared the master disk for each copy of the program you have, you can make backup and working copies with the usual DOS COPY and DISKCOPY commands.

However, don't try to copy anything until you've completed the prescribed first-time installation on the master disk. You could ruin your master disk, and copies of an uninstalled master will not run. Be sure you adhere exactly to the procedure described here.

Before you start the installation, be sure you can answer the questions about your hardware configuration that are mentioned in the steps that follow. However, except for your company name, you can change any of your answers later through the program's CCINSTAL utility.

1. Insert the Carbon Copy Plus master disk into a floppy disk drive (usually the A drive) and log on to that drive.

2. From the DOS prompt, type **CCSTART** and press **Enter**. You'll see a sign-on screen with a giant Carbon Copy Plus logo and a prompt telling you to enter your company name.

3. Type the name of your company carefully. It will appear on the control screen every time you run the program. You will not be permitted to run CCSTART a second time, so be sure the entry is the way you want it. If you make a mistake, type **N** when asked if the name is correct; then retype the name. When the entry is the way you want it, type **Y** to continue (see Figure 1.1).

Personal-izing your copy

Now the program will convert three command files stored with the .INS extension (for Install) into executable files you can actually use (with a new .EXE extension). These files are CC, CCHELP, and CCINSTAL. The screen will display a message: *Carbon Copy Customization Complete*. You're not through installing the master program disk at this point; the message refers only to your personalization of this copy of the program.

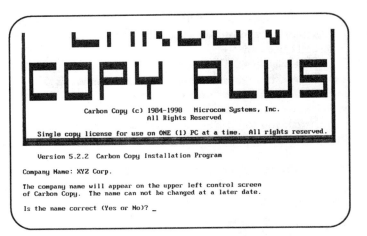

Figure 1.1: Identifying your company

Answering Basic Configuration Questions

Continue the installation by answering questions about your hardware.

1. The program asks whether you can read a welcome message clearly at the top of the screen. The purpose of this question is to determine whether or not you have a color monitor. Type **Y** for Yes if you have a color monitor; otherwise, type **N**.

2. The program next asks whether your screen is flickering or has "snow," a problem with some CGA monitors at their fastest screen-drawing speed. Type **Y** and your display will be adjusted to eliminate this interference. Type **N** if your display doesn't exhibit these symptoms. EGA and VGA monitors should not have these problems.

3. Now type a number from **1** through **4** to identify the serial port you'll use either to hard-wire your computer to another computer or to communicate by modem.

4. Modem type is the next item you need to define. (If computers will be wired together through a null modem cable, select the Direct Connect option.) Because space on the master disk is limited, the modem choices you'll see are limited too—mostly to models manufactured by Microcom, the publishers of Carbon Copy Plus (Figure 1.2). If you have a modem from another manufacturer—Hayes, for example—select AT Compatible as your modem; you can choose from 1200 baud, 2400 baud, or V.32 (9600 baud) speed. Later you'll have an opportunity to reselect your modem driver from a large list that probably includes your own modem's manufacturer and model.

5. You'll be prompted to select a speed for your modem. For example, if you have a fast, 9600-baud modem, but you'll always be communicating with slow, 1200-baud modems through Carbon Copy Plus, you might want to specify your speed as 1200. If you're using a direct-wired connection, select option A, for the maximum speed of 38.4K; in this case, the other computer

Temporary modem selection

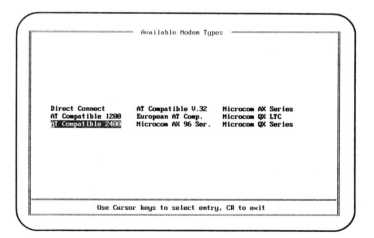

Figure 1.2: The initial modem selection list

with which you'll have contact must be set for the same speed.

At this point, you've completed the minimum installation of the program. You can type X to save the current configuration settings and then use Carbon Copy Plus immediately. A screen appears suggesting that you do just that. The program also presents another option that allows you to continue and configure the program in more detail, by pressing any key other than X. Later, you'll learn how to make additional modifications for special situations such as dialing through a company switchboard. You'll also learn how to incorporate security features and how to automate and customize the program so it will be easier to use.

For now, type X to save your answers to the installation questions. But before you use the program or configure it further, make a backup copy.

Backing Up the Program

You have finished the necessary customization of the master disk, so you can now successfully make a backup copy. If your copy of the program was provided on 360K 5.25-inch disks, you'll have a utility disk in addition to the master disk; back up both of them. If you're using the 3.5-inch disk format, the master and utility files are combined on a single 720K disk.

Backing Up a Floppy Disk System

If you have a floppy disk system, follow this routine:

1. Place a formatted blank disk in the B drive and an original Carbon Copy Plus disk in the A drive. (It's a good idea to write-protect your original disks at this point.)

2. From the A> prompt, type **COPY *.* B:** to copy each original disk in turn. The copies in your B drive will become your working disks.

3. Label the copies appropriately and store the originals in a safe place.

Copying the Program to a Hard Disk

If you have a hard disk, create a directory for the program there and copy the files from the floppy disks. The floppy disks will become your backup copies.

1. Log on to your hard disk and type **CD** and press **Enter**, to make sure you're at the root directory of that disk.

2. From the DOS prompt, type **MD CCPLUS** to make the directory for the program (of course, you could call the directory something other than CCPLUS—CCOPY or CARBON, for example).

3. Change to the new directory by typing **CD CCPLUS**.

4. Place your original disks (or copies) one by one into your A drive and type **COPY A:*.*** (unless, of course, the floppy disk drive you're using has some other letter designation). This command will transfer all of the files to your new hard disk directory.

5. Store the original disks for the program in a safe place.

If you have a previous version of Carbon Copy Plus on your hard disk, before you copy the new version onto your hard disk, erase all of the old-version files—except for configuration files (ending in .CFG) and script files (ending in .CCS), provided you want to retain those.

Step 2

Receiving Calls

15

Most people use Carbon Copy Plus to establish a connection with another computer for the purpose of giving or receiving help. The help could consist of a training session; for example, the person sitting at the keyboard of the guest computer at a remote location could operate the host PC to show a new employee how to use a word processor or spreadsheet program. On the other hand, the guest could run diagnostic tests to check the host's hard disk or change the setup of programs on the host system because of the recent installation of a new printer. The guest could even install additional software on the host PC from hundreds or thousands of miles away.

If you're the person in front of the host computer, your contributions to any of these functions will probably be simple:

1. Load Carbon Copy Plus into your computer's memory.
2. Watch your monitor as the person giving help runs your PC.
3. Ask questions, if necessary, by opening the chat window and typing your query (or type answers to questions from the guest).
4. End the session and remove Carbon Copy Plus from memory.

This Step discusses these host operations.

Setting Up to Receive a Call

Once Carbon Copy Plus has been installed, here's how to call up the program so a guest can log on to and operate your computer:

1. Change to the floppy disk drive or hard disk directory that contains the Carbon Copy Plus program files.

2. Type **CC** and press **Enter** to load the program.

3. Wait for the guest to call.

You'll see a message confirming that the program has now been installed into memory. This message will also show the key combination you must press to display menus (**Alt-RightShift**, unless someone has used advanced installation options to assign different "hot keys" to this function).

As the operator of a host computer, you probably won't need to use Carbon Copy Plus menus often. For example, the first option on the main menu (referred to as the control screen) allows you to press **F1** to call support. Most technical support departments place these data calls themselves, rather than asking the host operator to perform this function.

Furthermore, if you invoke the menus, either you or the operator of the guest PC must press **F10** to make the menus disappear before the remote user will be able to gain access to your computer.

Therefore, as a host, the best idea is usually to load Carbon Copy Plus into memory and not display any menus.

*What
you'll see
on your
screen*

So, assuming that you've loaded the program and haven't pressed the key combination to display the Carbon Copy Plus main menu, the first indication you'll have that the guest has dialed the number for your modem and has been connected to your computer will be the sight on your screen of activity that you didn't initiate. You may see commands magically appear to change drives or directories, list files, or start an application on your computer.

Asking a Question

If you want to ask the guest a question during a connect session, you can easily do so.

Here's all you have to do:

1. Press **Ctrl-RightShift** to display the chat window (unless someone has assigned another key combination to this function through the advanced installation options). The window will pop up in the top half of your screen, over any current application that's running. This same chat window also appears as a part of the main menu (or control screen) invoked with the **Alt-RightShift** keys.

2. Use the **Down Arrow** and **Up Arrow** keys to move the chat window from the top of the screen to the bottom or back up again, if you want to uncover a particular part of the underlying application screen so you can discuss it.

3. Type whatever you want to say to the support individual operating the guest PC. Your words will appear in the top half of the chat window, under the heading Your Dialogue. The guest's response will appear in the bottom half as Remote Operator's Dialogue. (The guest operator will see the positions and labels of these halves of the window reversed; what you've typed will appear on the monitor of the guest PC under Remote Operator's Dialogue.)

4. When you've finished the dialogue, either you or the remote operator can press **F10** to make the chat window disappear and to return to the application that was running.

The chat window is shown in Figure 2.1.

If both parties have telephones connected to their modems, you can also interrupt a data session by switching to voice mode. You can then actually talk by phone and then return again to data mode. This option is discussed in Step 6.

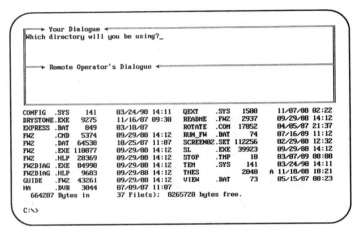

```
    → Your Dialogue ←
   Which directory will you be using?_


    → Remote Operator's Dialogue ←




  CONFIG  .SYS    141   03/24/90 14:11   QEXT     .SYS    1500    11/07/88 02:22
  DRYSTONE.EXE   9275   11/16/87 09:30   README   .FW2    2937    09/29/88 14:12
  EXPRESS .BAT    849   03/10/87         ROTATE   .COM   17052    04/05/87 21:37
  FW2     .CMD   5374   09/29/88 14:12   RUN_FW   .BAT      74    07/16/89 11:12
  FW2     .DAT  64538   10/25/87 11:07   SCREEN02.SET  112256    02/29/88 12:32
  FW2     .EXE 110877   09/29/88 14:12   SL       .EXE   39923    09/29/88 14:12
  FW2     .HLP  28369   09/29/88 14:12   STOP     .TMP      10    03/07/89 08:00
  FW2DIAG .EXE  84990   09/29/88 14:12   TEM      .SYS     141    03/24/90 14:11
  FW2DIAG .HLP   9603   09/29/88 14:12   THES             2048  A 11/18/88 10:21
  GUIDE   .FW2  43261   09/29/88 14:12   VIEW     .BAT      73    05/15/87 08:23
  HA      .DVR   3044   07/09/87 11:07
    664287 Bytes in      37 File(s);  8265728 bytes free.

  C:\>
```

Figure 2.1: Using the chat window

Terminating the Session

When a session has been completed, either party can terminate the connection.

1. Press **Alt-RightShift** to display the main menu or
    control screen.

2. Press **F1** to choose the first option, which, during a
    session, is Terminate Data Link.

3. Press **Enter** to confirm this choice (or **Esc** to cancel
    the selection, if you change your mind). You will now
    return to any application that was running on the host.

4. To remove Carbon Copy Plus from memory (thereby
    freeing the 61K RAM it occupies), return to the DOS
    prompt, change to the Carbon Copy Plus directory
    if necessary by typing **CD\CCPLUS**, and then type
    CCREMOVE. You'll see the screen shown in Fig-
    ure 2.2.

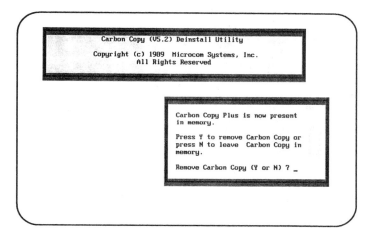

Figure 2.2: Removing Carbon Copy Plus from memory

5. Type **Y** to remove the program from memory (or **N** to cancel removal). You won't see a confirming message.

Step 3

Making Calls

 15

When you're the operator of a guest computer using Carbon Copy Plus, you'll probably be calling a host PC to provide help by temporarily taking over the control of that computer. Even the name of the guest module—CCHELP—reflects this role.

Recall that, for your computer to function as a host, you type the command **CC** to load Carbon Copy Plus into memory; then you wait for calls. When you're the individual who's going to make the calls and provide support, you activate a different module of Carbon Copy Plus named CCHELP.

When you complete this step, along with Steps 1 and 2, you will know the bare-bones actions necessary to use Carbon Copy Plus either as a host or guest.

Placing the Call

Here's how you make the connection with the host computer:

1. Change to the drive or hard disk directory that contains the Carbon Copy Plus program.

2. From the DOS prompt, type **CCHELP** and press **Enter**. You'll see the initial screen followed by the control screen or main menu shown in Figure 3.1.

3. Press **F1** to select the first option, Call CC User. You'll be prompted to enter the number you want to call. (If the computers are wired together, you won't need to type a telephone number; press **F1** and then press **Enter** immediately. The connection should be made instantly, and you'll be asked for a password.)

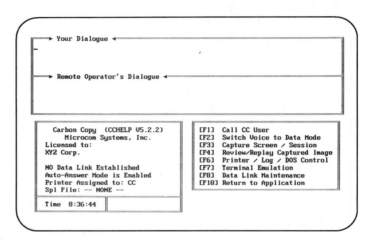

```
    ┌──▶ Your Dialogue ◀════════════════════════════════════════
  ─ │
    └──▶ Remote Operator's Dialogue ◀════════════════════════════

┌─────────────────────────────────┐ ┌──────────────────────────────┐
│   Carbon Copy  (CCHELP V5.2.2)  │ │ [F1]  Call CC User           │
│      Microcom Systems, Inc.     │ │ [F2]  Switch Voice to Data Mode │
│  Licensed to:                   │ │ [F3]  Capture Screen / Session │
│  XYZ Corp.                      │ │ [F4]  Review/Replay Captured Image │
│                                 │ │ [F6]  Printer / Log / DOS Control │
│  NO Data Link Established       │ │ [F7]  Terminal Emulation     │
│  Auto-Answer Mode is Enabled    │ │ [F8]  Data Link Maintenance  │
│  Printer Assigned to: CC        │ │ [F10] Return to Application  │
│  Spl File: -- NONE --           │ │                              │
├─────────────────────────────────┤ └──────────────────────────────┘
│  Time  8:36:44  │               │
└─────────────────┴───────────────┘
```

Figure 3.1: The guest's menu before the operator makes a call

4. Type the phone number and press **Enter**. (If a call table has been set up, you can pick the location to call by its name, such as Memphis Branch Office. You'll learn how to create a call table in Step 4.) A message will appear telling you that the number is being dialed. When the host computer answers, you'll be asked for a password, as shown in Figure 3.2. (If you dialed through a call table, the appropriate password will be transmitted automatically; you won't be prompted for it.)

5. Unless a special password has been established in the host's password table (password tables are discussed in Step 5), you'll use the default Carbon Copy Plus password, CC. Type **CC** now (the password you type will not appear on the screen) and press **Enter**. The status window in the lower-left area of your control screen will change to display the message *Data Link is Established.*

6. Unless you want to start the session by using the chat window to communicate with the operator of the host

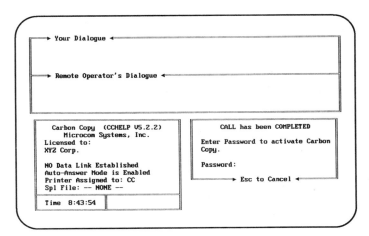

Carbon Copy (CCHELP V5.2.2)
      Microcom Systems, Inc.
Licensed to:
XYZ Corp.

NO Data Link Established
Auto-Answer Mode is Enabled
Printer Assigned to: CC
Spl File: -- NONE --

Time 8:43:54

CALL has been COMPLETED

Enter Password to activate Carbon
Copy.

Password:

Esc to Cancel

Figure 3.2: Entering the password for the host

PC, press **F10** to remove the control screen from your monitor.

You'll now see the same information displayed that the host operator will see: probably a DOS prompt indicating that the active host directory is the one where Carbon Copy Plus is installed (and the one from where the CC module was loaded). Unless you're using a password with restricted privileges (the default password CC has no restrictions), you can now operate the host computer as if you were sitting in front of it. You can run any program, create directories, erase files, or even install a new application by remote control (once you learn about another module, called CCDOS).

To return to the control screen at any time, just press **Alt-RightShift** (unless someone has assigned that function to another key combination). The menu options should be those shown in Figure 3.3.

You can always return to the control screen

In the same manner described for the host computer in Step 2, you can also display only the chat window of the control

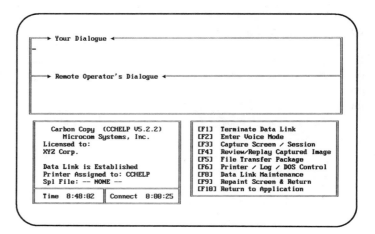

Figure 3.3: The guest control screen during a session

screen by pressing **Ctrl-RightShift** and then pressing the **Down Arrow** or **Up Arrow** key to reposition the chat window on the screen so you can see either the top or bottom half of an application screen underneath it. Press **F10** to make the screen disappear and return to the application.

Ending the Session

Although either party can end the session, normally the guest will initiate this action.

1. Press **Alt-RightShift** to pop up the control screen.

2. Press **F1** to select the first option, Terminate Data Link.

3. Press **Enter** to confirm your decision (or **Esc** if you change your mind).

You won't have to issue a command to remove the CCHELP module from memory, because—unlike the CC module used on host computers—CCHELP does not remain in RAM after a Carbon Copy Plus session has been terminated. You'll be operating your own (the guest) computer again.

If an application was running on the host when the connection was terminated, it will continue to run. Also, any batch processing will continue. In fact, as a guest, you can log on to the host again later to see how the batch job is progressing.

Step 4

Making Calls Automatically

15

Although Carbon Copy Plus can function after you've finished installing the master disk, you'll probably want some
additional capabilities right away. In particular, you'll soon
get tired of looking up phone numbers and passwords all the
time in order to call other computers. As indicated in Step 3,
you can automate the dialing process by setting up a call table
of frequently called numbers. To accomplish this goal, you
use the program's CCINSTAL module to change or add to the
configuration choices you made in Step 1.

While you're making changes, you should make sure that you're
using the correct driver for your particular brand and type of
modem.

Adding a Longer List of Modems

If the installation menu did not include your modem, your
first action should be to replace that short list of modems with
a much longer one that is stored on the program's utility disk.
The file that contains this list is called MODEM.DSC. If you
have a hard disk and copied the contents of both Carbon
Copy Plus disks to your CCPLUS directory, the file will already be available.

If you have a floppy disk system, you'll have to copy the
MODEM.DSC file from your utility disk to the working copy
of the master disk. Then erase the file called MODEM.DSS
from that disk (or, if you're using a hard disk, from your
CCPLUS directory). MODEM.DDS contains the short list of
modems that you won't be using anymore.

Now you're ready to enter the CCINSTAL module.

Selecting Your Modem and Other General Parameters

On a floppy disk system, CCINSTAL will be on the working copy of your master disk. Log on to the drive that contains that disk and, from the DOS prompt, type **CCINSTAL** and press **Enter**.

If Carbon Copy Plus is on your hard disk, change to your hard disk directory, type **CCINSTAL**, and press **Enter**.

You'll see the System Parameters screen shown in Figure 4.1.

The System Parameter screen lets you change the configuration you set up during the installation of the master disk. You can assign a new Comm port or change the baud rate, type of display, and other general parameters.

Option C is Modem Type. You use this option to activate the driver for a modem other than Microcom and generic AT-compatible models.

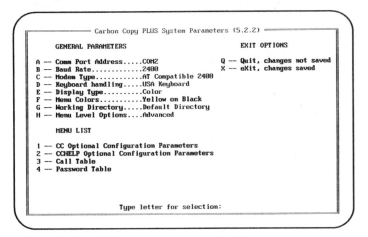

```
═══════ Carbon Copy PLUS System Parameters (5.2.2) ═══════

  GENERAL PARAMETERS                         EXIT OPTIONS

A -- Comm Port Address.....COM2         Q -- Quit, changes not saved
B -- Baud Rate.............2400         X -- eXit, changes saved
C -- Modem Type............AT Compatible 2400
D -- Keyboard handling.....USA Keyboard
E -- Display Type..........Color
F -- Menu Colors...........Yellow on Black
G -- Working Directory.....Default Directory
H -- Menu Level Options....Advanced

  MENU LIST

1 -- CC Optional Configuration Parameters
2 -- CCHELP Optional Configuration Parameters
3 -- Call Table
4 -- Password Table




              Type letter for selection:
```

Figure 4.1: The System Parameters screen

1. To change the specified modem, type **C**. You'll imme-
    diately see a long list of modems similar to the one
    shown in Figure 4.2.

2. Use the cursor keys to highlight the name of your mo-
    dem. Then press **Enter**. If your modem is not listed,
    select one that you know is compatible with yours.

3. You'll be returned to the System Parameters screen.
    Your modem should now be listed under option C.

4. Make any other changes you want in the General
    Parameters section of the screen. If you answered
    the questions correctly during the installation of the
    master disk, you probably won't need to change these
    items now.

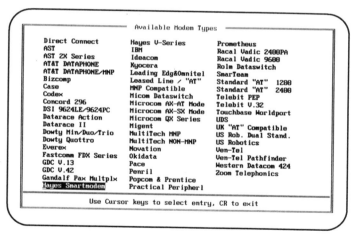

Figure 4.2: The list of modems supported

Getting Familiar with the Call Table

You access the call table from the System Parameters screen
by selecting Call Table, option 1 in the Menu List section of
the screen.

The pass-word is sent auto-matically

Figure 4.3 shows what the call table looks like before it is configured.

Note that the top of the table screen displays function key assignments that you can use in conjunction with entries into the table. Below the function key area are three initially empty columns where you can enter the names of remote facilities to be contacted, along with the phone number and the password that is required to access each. Once you've entered data in these columns, you can highlight a name to call. The number will then be dialed automatically.

If you are at the keyboard of the guest computer (using the CCHELP module), the password in this table will be transmitted to the host system (the computer that is using the CC module and is waiting for your assistance).

If you're operating the host computer and call the guest for help, no password is required.

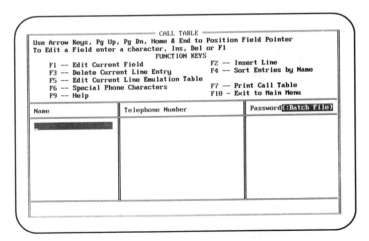

Figure 4.3: The call table before configuration

Passwords for the host computer are set through a separate password table that is explained in Step 5. Separate passwords and clearance levels can be established for individual callers.

Filling In the Call Table

To move around the call table, you can use any of the following keys: the cursor arrows, **PgUp, PgDn, Home,** and **End.** Once the cursor is in a field, you can edit it by simply starting to type or by pressing **Ins, Del,** or **F1** (the **F1** function key merely places the field in edit mode).

Keys you can use

Other function key assignments that are available include **F2** to insert a line at the cursor position in the call table, **F3** to delete the current line entry, **F4** to sort all of the line entries by name (they're sorted automatically anyway when you leave the call table), **F5** to store a terminal emulator configuration (discussed in a later step), **F6** to enter special phone characters (you'll learn more about this option shortly), **F7** to print a copy of the call table, **F9** to access a help screen, and **F10** to exit to the main menu.

1. Begin preparing your call table by placing the cursor in the Name field.

2. Type a name for the first remote computer you want to contact. This name can consist of any identifying words that will be meaningful to you and others who may be using your system. The name must begin with a letter and cannot be longer than 19 characters. Also, it cannot contain any spaces. To separate words, use the underline character instead of a space. Press **Enter** to move to the next field.

3. Type the telephone number to be called, including the area code. For readability, you can insert dashes and parentheses, but the program needs only the digits in order to function.

4. Very few modem connections require the use of special characters in dialing, but provision has been made for these too. For example, if you must go through a switchboard to place an outgoing call and must dial 9 to access an outside line, you may need to insert a pause after the 9 to allow time for the switchboard to make the outside connection. You can press **F6** while in the Telephone Number field of the call table to access a window that lists special characters you can add to send a line feed, wait for a carrier detect, insert a carriage return, or place a half-second delay in the dialing sequence (see Figure 4.4). In this case, you would select the delay option. A tilde (~) appears in the Telephone Number field to represent this feature. If you need a pause longer than half a second, select the option more than once.

(You can also insert dial modifiers, which are other characters added to the Telephone Number field for special purposes: A comma produces a 2-second pause, and a P tells the program to pulse-dial the number that follows.)

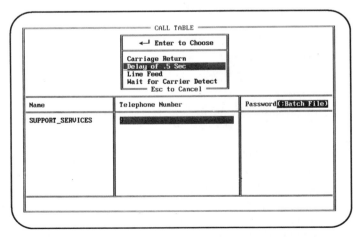

Figure 4.4: Adding special characters to a phone number

5. Press **Enter** to move to the Password field.

6. Type a password. The password must be 16 characters or less and contain no spaces. Any password entered here to call a host computer must also be entered in the password table of the host computer. Your completed call table might look like Figure 4.5.

A pass-word must also be in a host's password table

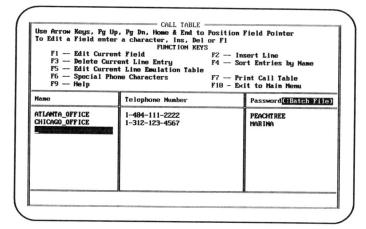

```
═══════════ CALL TABLE ═══════════
Use Arrow Keys, Pg Up, Pg Dn, Home & End to Position Field Pointer
To Edit a Field enter a character, Ins, Del or F1
                        FUNCTION KEYS
    F1 -- Edit Current Field           F2 -- Insert Line
    F3 -- Delete Current Line Entry     F4 -- Sort Entries by Name
    F5 -- Edit Current Line Emulation Table
    F6 -- Special Phone Characters      F7 -- Print Call Table
    F9 -- Help                          F10 - Exit to Main Menu

 Name              │ Telephone Number    │ Password(:Batch File)

 ATLANTA_OFFICE    │ 1-404-111-2222      │ PEACHTREE
 CHICAGO_OFFICE    │ 1-312-123-4567      │ MARINA
```

Figure 4.5: A completed call table

7. When you've finished the call table, press **F10** to return to the main System Parameters menu. If you want to stop configuring Carbon Copy Plus at this point, press **X** from this menu to save your work and exit CCINSTAL.

Now, from the initial control screen you see when you load either the CC or the CCHELP module, you can press **F1** (*Call CC User*), and you'll find that the names you've entered in the call table are ready for selection and automatic dialing (see Figure 4.6).

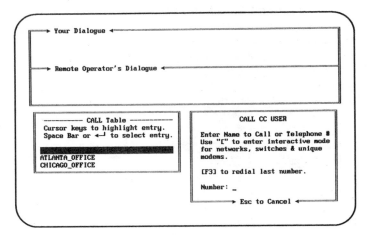

Figure 4.6: Dialing from the call table

Most companies these days are concerned about security in their computer operations. You've already learned about one security feature of this program: You must enter a password to obtain access to a host PC. As already explained, all copies of Carbon Copy Plus are shipped with a default password: CC. This default password makes the program operational immediately with minimum knowledge on the part of the users. However, this ease of use also means that unauthorized people can easily gain access to a host computer through the default password.

The solution, of course, is to establish your own passwords as soon as possible, using the call table discussed in Step 4 plus the password table.

You reach the password table through CCINSTAL by selecting option 4 on the System Parameters menu.

Only a computer serving as a host can use the password table. On this table you can enter up to 63 passwords for separate callers, each with an individually specified access level.

You can provide additional security by having the host computer automatically hang up after a caller gives a valid password and then call back the telephone number specified for the guest who has been assigned that password.

Using the Password Table

Figure 5.1 shows the initial settings for the password table.

Note that the default password table shows CC as the only current password. The second column, which is empty, is where you can specify a callback phone number. The third

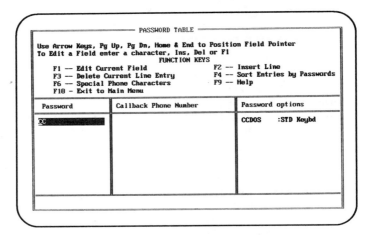

Figure 5.1: The default password table

column, Password Options, is where you specify the access level and other information related to the password. The access level in this field now is CCDOS, the highest level, meaning that a guest using the CC password is allowed to perform any operation on the host computer.

The Password Options field also displays the notation *:STD Keybd*. The default table assumes that the caller is using a standard keyboard. You can change this specification if you're using a terminal emulation board, as will be explained later.

Navigating the table

To navigate the password table, you use the same keys (arrow keys, **PgDn**, and so on) that you used with the call table.

The function key assignments that are active for the password table include **F1** to edit the current field, **F2** to insert a line, **F3** to delete the current line entry, **F4** to sort the entered lines by password (they're sorted automatically when you exit to the main menu), **F6** to enter the special phone characters described for this function key in Step 2, **F9** to display a help screen, and **F10** to exit to the main menu.

Establishing Passwords

Here's how you set up passwords:

1. Move to the first column (the Password column) and write over the default password, CC, with a new entry. As in the call table, the password cannot exceed 16 characters, and it must not include spaces. Press **Enter** to move to the second column, where you can enter a callback phone number. If you don't intend to use this feature, press **Enter** again to move to the last column.

If you want to use the program's automatic background file transfer feature in conjunction with a guest, that guest's password must have the highest access level (see action 4 that follows) and must be linked in the call table to the name of an existing CCDOS batch file (CCDOS is a Carbon Copy Plus feature and not a function of the DOS operating system). CCDOS and automatic background transfer are discussed in later Steps.

2. If you want the additional protection of the program's callback capability, enter the phone number of the guest PC in the second column. As in the call table, you can type dashes and parentheses for greater legibility and enter special phone characters by pressing **F6**.

Before you use the callback feature, you must go to the main System Parameters menu, select option 1 to reach the CC Optional Configuration Parameters submenu, and then select option K (Call Back). Selecting Call Back automatically changes the word No entered in the field to Yes and activates the callback feature.

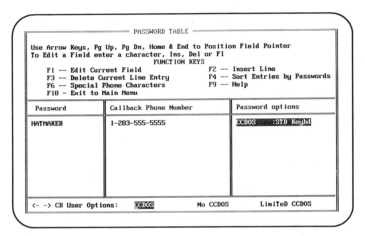

Figure 5.2: Setting the guest's access level

3. You do no typing in the third column of the password table. Once you've entered the field, press **Enter** to display the security-level options. You can pick one of three access levels (see Figure 5.2).

Assigning access levels

4. CCDOS is the highest access level. This level allows the remote guest to create directories, copy or erase files, and perform any other function on the host PC. If you limit the caller's access to Limited CCDOS, the guest can perform functions only in the directory the host is using when the guest establishes contact. Under Limited CCDOS, the guest cannot delete or rename files, and background file transfers cannot be performed (such transfers are discussed in a later Step). The third and most restricted level, No CCDOS, has the same limitations as Limited CCDOS, except that no foreground file transfers can be performed either. Highlight your selection and press **Enter**. You'll move to a new line, where you can specify the information for another password.

5. After you've completed the password list for guest callers, press **F10** to exit the submenu and (if you're ready to leave the CCINSTAL module) type **X** to save your changes.

You can now use Carbon Copy Plus with the convenience of a call table and the security of your own passwords.

Hiding the Call and Password Tables

For added security, you can hide the call and password tables so the options to access them will not appear on the CCIN-STAL menus. You do this on the password table. Merely move the cursor to an empty line and type a tilde (~) in the password field, followed by a special security password, like this: **~MYWORD** (as with other passwords, special security passwords can consist of a maximum of 16 characters, with no spaces permitted). Then press **Enter**. There's no need to fill in the Callback Phone Number or Password Options fields. Regardless of the line you were on, the security password will be stored in the last row of the table.

After you establish a special security password, when you run CCINSTAL you'll have to type the tilde and the password from the main System Parameters menu in order to make the call and password tables visible and usable. If you access the password table, you'll also have to press the **End** key if you want to make the security password itself temporarily visible.

If you decide to use a security password to hide the call and password tables from prying eyes, don't forget what it is!

You can recover from the problem of a forgotten password, but you will lose all of the custom configuring you've done. If the program has been loaded, remove it from memory by typing **CCREMOVE D** from the DOS prompt and then pressing **Enter**. Then erase the files in your Carbon Copy

Plus directory that end with the extension .CFG and enter CCINSTAL and type **X** to exit, even though you've made no changes. New .CFG files will be created with the program's default settings, and you'll see the call and password tables listed on your main menu again. Of course, you'll have to fill out the tables again from scratch.

You've learned that you can use the chat window to type messages to the operator of a remote computer during a Carbon Copy Plus connect session, and that this individual can also type responses in the corresponding chat window of the remote computer. However, if you need to have a long conversation, you may feel that typing messages isn't adequate. In that case, you can switch from data to voice mode and talk to the remote operator on the telephone.

Of course, you can't talk by telephone if one of you doesn't have a phone connected to your modem, if one of the modems doesn't support voice operations (rare today), or if the two machines are direct-wired and use no modems or telephones. In fact, if the PCs are connected by a null modem cable, the switching function option (**F2**) does not appear on the control screen menu.

CCHELP is automatically configured for voice mode before you call a host. (**F2** on the control screen menu at this point says Switch Voice to Data Mode.) However, if you don't pick up a phone attached to your modem when the number dialed starts ringing, you'll be switched to data mode automatically as a PC running CC in data mode accepts the call.

Getting Past a Switchboard

Sometimes you may want to use the default voice mode configuration as you call a host: for instance, when you must go through a company switchboard to reach the host's data line. Just pick up the phone as soon as the number dialed starts ringing. You'll be in voice mode, and you can ask for the extension you want. Then, when you hear the answer tone of the host's modem as you're connected to that extension, press **F2** to switch back to data mode.

Most users of Carbon Copy Plus won't have to go through a switchboard to reach a host data line and will normally use the capability of switching between data and voice modes only to talk with a remote operator after a data connection has been established.

Starting a Conversation

Here are the actions involved in starting a conversation:

1. If you want to speak to the operator of the remote computer, press **Alt-RightShift** to display the control screen. Then press **F2** to switch to voice mode. You'll see the message shown in Figure 6.1: *ACTIVATE VOICE MODE. Remote User has been notified that you want to talk. Please wait for acknowledgment before picking up the telephone.*

2. The operator of the remote computer will see a different message: *VOICE MODE REQUESTED. Remote*

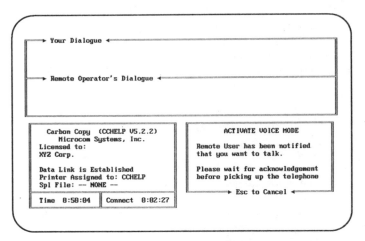

```
┌───► Your Dialogue ◄──────────────────────────────────────┐
│                                                           │
│                                                           │
├───► Remote Operator's Dialogue ◄──────────────────────────┤
│                                                           │
│                                                           │
│  ┌──────────────────────────┐ ┌─────────────────────────┐ │
│  │ Carbon Copy (CCHELP V5.2.2)│ │    ACTIVATE VOICE MODE   │ │
│  │    Microcom Systems, Inc. │ │                         │ │
│  │ Licensed to:             │ │ Remote User has been notified│ │
│  │ XYZ Corp.                │ │ that you want to talk.  │ │
│  │                          │ │                         │ │
│  │ Data Link is Established │ │ Please wait for acknowledgement│ │
│  │ Printer Assigned to: CCHELP│ │ before picking up the telephone│ │
│  │ Spl File: -- NONE --     │ │                         │ │
│  │                          │ │    ► Esc to Cancel ◄    │ │
│  │ Time  8:58:04 │ Connect 0:02:27│ └─────────────────────────┘ │
│  └──────────────────────────┘                            │
└───────────────────────────────────────────────────────────┘
```

Figure 6.1: Control screen after the operator presses F2 for voice mode

*User asks to talk. To accept, press Enter. To reject,
press Esc. Please wait for acknowledgment before
picking up the telephone.* The remote operator now
either presses **Enter** to talk or **Esc** to reject the request.
You might ask, why would someone reject a request to
talk? The host probably wouldn't; but if the request
was generated by the host and you happen to be the
operator of the guest PC and in the middle of some
procedure that you want to complete, you might well
want to say, in effect, "Later!"

3. If the remote operator presses **Esc**, the request is can-
celed, and the normal control screen is displayed again.
If the remote operator presses **Enter**, the next message
you'll see is the one in Figure 6.2: *VOICE MODE
ENABLED. Pick up the telephone then press any key to
quiet the modem.*

4. Both parties then pick up their receivers and have their
conversation. As shown in Figure 6.3, the control
screen message now says, *VOICE MODE. Press [F2]
to return to Data Mode.*

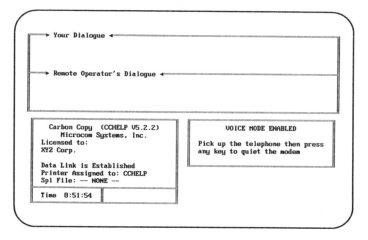

Figure 6.2: Control screen after remote operator agrees to talk

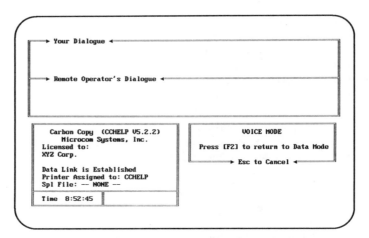

Figure 6.3: Control screen during voice mode conversation

Returning to Data Mode

Either party can press **F2** to end the conversation and return to data mode. But don't hang up until both sides have pressed **F2**; otherwise, Carbon Copy Plus will immediately terminate the connection.

Switching back to data mode shouldn't catch either party by surprise because the intent to issue this command would normally be mentioned in the telephone conversation before voice mode is discontinued.

It's not likely that the request to start voice mode will be missed by the other operator either, because the control screen must be displayed before voice mode can be initiated, and—as we've seen—the request appears prominently in the lower-right area of that screen, replacing the normal menu options.

Nevertheless, if you're the person who has asked for a voice contact, you should not be surprised if a slight delay occurs before you get a response. After all, no audible alert is issued. Particularly on the host end of the connection, where little activity is required of the operator, the other party may be looking at something else in the room or may even have stepped away from the computer for a moment.

In most cases, you will find switching modes easy to do and a real convenience.

You have several options for recording information about Carbon Copy Plus sessions. You can create a log that identifies each computer that makes contact with you; this log includes dates and times as well as the files and directories accessed. You can also log the activities on your own computer before and after the connection is made.

Carbon Copy Plus offers visual alternatives too. You can take a "snapshot" of any single screen displayed during a session, you can set up the program to capture all of the screens in a session automatically.

First we'll explore the logging options. To use this feature, you use the CCINSTAL module introduced in Step 4 and change a default program setting.

Establishing a Log File

Carbon Copy Plus is shipped with its session-logging capabilities disabled. Here's how to change this.

1. Log on to the drive or hard-disk directory that contains Carbon Copy Plus.

2. From the DOS prompt, type **CCINSTAL** to load the installation module. Press **Enter**. You'll see the System Parameters screen, or main menu, that was introduced in Figure 4.1.

Although some parameters apply only to the CC module or the CCHELP module, the Log File option is what is called a common parameter—a parameter that can be used in both the CC and CCHELP modules. You can change a common parameter by accessing either the CC or CCHELP Optional Configuration Parameters submenu.

3. Type **1** to display the CC Optional Configuration Parameters submenu. This menu is shown in Figure 7.1.

4. Press **E** to change the Log File setting to the one you want. Each time you press **E**, you will see another Log File option, until the cycle returns to the default selection, None, and then starts over again. Here are your choices:

You can choose how much activity to log

• None, of course, means that none of your Carbon Copy Plus activities will be recorded.

• Logging On & Off Only records the time that a connection is made and terminated, plus the total elapsed time, the caller's identity, and the caller's Carbon Copy Plus serial number.

• Full Logging & File Operations provides all of the features of the Logging On & Off Only option and, in addition, records all files and directories accessed during the connection.

```
============ CC Optional Configuration Parameters ============

     CC and CCHELP Common Parameters          F10 -- Exit to Main Menu

A -- Normal Modem Mode.....Answer     H -- Keystroke Processing..Fast
B -- Answer Ring Count.....Default    I -- Modem Reset..........Full
C -- Redial Attempts.......None
D -- Redial Delay..........None
E -- Log File..............None
F -- Startup Keystrokes....<ALT><RIGHT-SHIFT>
G -- Dial Time Out.........1 Minute, 30 Seconds

     CC Parameters

J -- Reboot on Exit........No
K -- Call Back.............No
L -- Password Attempts.....Unlimited
M -- Chat Keystrokes.......<CTRL><RIGHT-SHIFT>
N -- Inactivity Time-Out...Unlimited
O -- Usage Time-Out........Unlimited


              Type letter for selection:
```

Figure 7.1: The CC configuration parameters submenu

- Continuous Audit creates the most comprehensive log, but this option slows down operations on the PC noticeably, unless you're using a very fast computer. This option records all files and directories accessed from the moment the CC or CCHELP module is loaded into memory, regardless of whether a connection has been made with another computer.

Because it logs the identity of callers with their serial numbers, the Logging On and Off Only option can help you spot possible security breaches. The time and duration information that this option also records for the session can help you analyze the amount of time spent in technical support activities, as well as the amount of support required by the operators of individual computers. However, the Full Logging & File Operations option is even more useful for both purposes because, in addition, it logs all files and directories accessed, thus helping you recall what activities were performed during the connect session. Continuous Audit hinders the performance of the computer and adds to the features of the Full Logging option only a record of disk accesses before and after the connect session—a record usually of little value, unless you feel that you must have a continuous audit of all activity. Therefore, Full Logging is the most sensible choice for most operations.

5. After you've made your choice, press **F10** to return to the main menu and **X** to save your modification and return to the DOS prompt.

The log file will be named CC.LOG. It will be activated automatically every time you use either the CC or CCHELP module on your computer for a connect session.

Using the Log File

Through a separate utility called CCLOG, you can view the
log file, print it, or even delete it. Here's how to use this
utility:

1. Type **CCLOG** at the DOS prompt of your Carbon
    Copy Plus directory. Then press **Enter**. You'll see the
    menu shown in Figure 7.2.

The first option on this menu, Name of Log File, seems to indicate that you can rename the log file something other than
CC.LOG. The manual describes how to do this and even says
you can store the log file on another disk or in another directory by inserting a path before the file name. However, as of
the date when this book was written, this feature had not yet
been implemented. So unless you're using some later version
of Carbon Copy Plus that corrects this situation, be fore-
warned that the Name of Log File option does not work, and

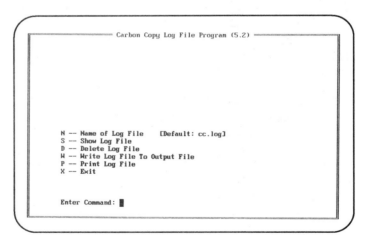

Figure 7.2: The file menu

you cannot rename the log file or use it anywhere except in your regular Carbon Copy Plus directory. This "bug" is no real disadvantage to most users; the default name CC.LOG should be adequate.

2. Type **S** to select Show Log File if you want to view the contents of an existing log file. Log files are stored in a proprietary format, so you must use this menu option to read your log—unless you want to take advantage of other choices on the menu to create a disk file in ASCII format or send the file to your printer. As shown in Figure 7.3, the file is recorded and displayed in four columns:

How the log is displayed

- The first column, Type, specifies the kind of activity that is being reported.

- The second column, Date/Time, lists the month and day of the session. This column is filled in only when each session starts and ends.

```
══════════════ Carbon Copy Log File ══════════════
F10 - Return to Menu        Home, End, PgUp, PgDn, Up, Down - View Log File

  TYPE      DATE/TIME          ID/SN                     REFERENCE
 ───────  ──────────────   ─────────────────    ─────────────────────────

Login    APR 15  11:10    03000054              XYZ Corp.
  Change Directory         \
  Change Directory         C:\
  Open File                C:\BATCH\DEB.BAT
  Open File                C:\BATCH\DEB.BAT
  Open File                C:\BATCH\DEB.BAT
  Open File                C:\BATCH\DEB.BAT
  Change Directory         \dataease
  Open File                C:\BATCH\DEB.BAT
  Open File                DEASE.EXE
  Open File                C:\DATAEASE\DEMAINTC.OVL
  Open File                configur.dat
  Open File                demessag.msg
  Open File                C:\DATAEASE\DEASE.EXE
  Change Directory         C:\DATAEASE
  Change Directory         C:\DATAEASE
  Open File                C:\DATAEASE\DELNGENG.OVL
  Open File                ztermdef.dbz
```

Figure 7.3: Reading a log file

- The third column, ID/SN, shows the serial number of the calling computer at login time, plus any special identification that is typed in when a file is annotated (annotation is explained later in this Step). This column also lists the directories and files accessed (if either the Full Logging or Continuous Audit option has been activated).

- The fourth column, Reference, shows the elapsed time in days, hours, and minutes and is also where file annotations appear.

You can use the **Home, End, PgUp, PgDn,** and **Up** and **Down Arrow** keys to navigate the log file screen. To exit the log file screen, you press **F10**.

3. To erase the log file, press **D** to select the Delete Log File option. You'll be asked to confirm your action by typing **Y**; type **N** if you change your mind.

4. To create an ASCII file from the log information, press **W** for Write Log File to Output File. You'll be asked for a file name. Type a file name. Then press **Enter**.

5. To send the log file to your printer, press **P** for Print Log File. Be sure the printer is on line and ready, because no confirmation is requested for this command; the program executes it immediately.

6. Type **X** to exit the CCLOG utility and return to the DOS prompt.

Adding Notes to Your Log File

Although the log file can show every directory and file accessed, it doesn't show why the file was accessed. For example, as illustrated by Figure 7.3, the execution of a batch file is recorded only as several consecutive accesses of the same file. Fortunately, you can add notes to the log file to indicate what was actually accomplished during a session.

Here is the procedure to follow:

1. Any time during a session that you want to annotate the log file, press **F6** from the CCHELP main menu to reach the Printer/Log/DOS Control submenu. If you're using the CC module instead, the submenu is called Printer/Log Control.

2. Press **1** for Enter Log File Data. You'll see the data entry window shown in Figure 7.4.

3. On the first line of this window, the ID line, you can type up to 29 characters to identify the session. (The ID line is a good place to list the name of the person making the support call and to identify the call in any other way.) Whatever you type will appear in capital letters. Press **Enter** to move to the second line.

4. On the second line, the Ref line, you can enter another 29 letters. Again, your entry will appear in all capital letters. The Ref line is a good place to describe the task

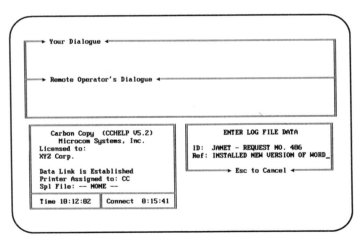

Figure 7.4: Adding a note to a log file

performed. When you press **Enter** this time, the contents of the two lines will be added to the log file, and you will be returned to the main menu.

Whenever you add a note to a log file, here's the way it will actually appear in the file:

- The note will appear in the log file on one line.

- The first column (Type) will display the word *Informational*.

- The second column (Date/Time) will be blank.

- The third column (ID/SN) will display the identification you entered on the first line of the data entry window.

- The fourth column (Reference) will display the text you entered on the second line of the data entry window.

You can't write very much information when you can enter only 29 characters. If you need more words than you can squeeze into that space to describe the accomplishments of your session, simply return to the Carbon Copy Plus main menu and add a second, third, or fourth note immediately after the first.

Capturing a Screen or an Entire Session

When you're trying to discover the nature of an operational problem on a host computer, it is helpful to have a record of exactly what transpires when the PC is in use. You can get such a record by using the Capture Screen/Session option (F3; called simply Capture Screen Image on host computers) on the main menu. Although on a host computer you can capture only a single screen at a time with this feature, when you operate your PC as a guest, you can record all of the screen images in an entire connect session.

On either host or guest, you press **F3** and then enter a file name to save the current screen. The program automatically adds the .CAP extension to the name you choose. On the guest you can type **/P** after the file name to capture all screen changes in the session, as shown in Figure 7.5.

On either the host or guest, you press **F4** and enter a file name to view a captured screen. On the guest PC, if the file name represents a session capture, the program automatically displays the screens from the session, one after the other in the order in which they were created. You can hold down the **Left Arrow** key to slow down the presentation or hold down the **Right Arrow** key to speed it up. Press the space bar to pause or restart the sequence.

You press **Esc** to end the show and then any key to return to the main menu.

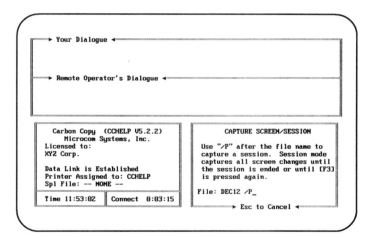

Figure 7.5: Capturing all screens from a session

Local & Remote Printing

Output from an application running on a host PC during a connect session normally goes to a printer connected to the host. However, you can also direct the output to both the host and guest printers, to the guest printer only, to a spool file on the guest computer, or to both the guest printer and a guest spool file.

Spool files in Carbon Copy Plus save the application output for printing later through a specific DeSpool command. Only a computer functioning as a guest can use spool files.

In the CCHELP (guest) module, you can make initial printing choices by using the CCINSTAL installation utility (discussed in this Step) and then select other options during your connect session (see Step 9). However, in the CC (host) module, you have fewer printing options, and these can be changed only during the connect session.

Choosing Printing Default Settings

Here's how to change CCHELP printing default settings using CCINSTAL:

1. Change to the disk or directory that contains your Carbon Copy Plus program files, type **CCINSTAL**, and press **Enter**.

2. From the System Parameters screen that the program displays, select item 2, CCHELP Optional Configuration Parameters. You'll now see the screen shown in Figure 8.1. Item P on this screen is Printer Assignment. Printer Assignment has two options: CC (the default selection) directs output to the host printer; CCHELP directs output to the guest printer.

3. Press **P** if necessary to toggle the Printer Assignment parameter between CC and CCHELP to display the setting you want.

If you pick CC, the Initial Spool File option (Item S, described below) must be set to None. If you select CCHELP, the Initial Spool File option must be set to a choice other than None.

The program offers partial automatic protection from selecting the wrong combination of these options. If item S, Initial Spool File, is not set to None, you will be unable to change the Printer Assignment from CCHELP to CC (because, as already mentioned, spool files are not supported on a computer serving as a host). On the other hand, if Printer Assignment is already set to CC and you press **S** to change the spool file item from None to something else, the Printer Assignment parameter will automatically switch from CC to CCHELP.

The one situation in which you must choose the right combination of the P and S items yourself is when the menu already

```
================= CCHELP Optional Configuration Parameters =================

     CC and CCHELP Common Parameters           F10 -- Exit to Main Menu

 A -- Normal Modem Mode.....Answer    H -- Keystroke Processing..Fast
 B -- Answer Ring Count.....Default   I -- Modem Reset..........Full
 C -- Redial Attempts.......03
 D -- Redial Delay..........30 Seconds
 E -- Log File..............Full Logging & File Operations
 F -- Startup Keystrokes....<ALT><RIGHT-SHIFT>
 G -- Dial Time Out.........1 Minute, 30 Seconds

     CCHELP Parameters

 P -- Printer Assignment....CC
 Q -- Synchronized Mode.....Enabled
 R -- Graphics Display......Full
 S -- Initial Spool File....None



              Type letter for selection:
```

Figure 8.1: The CCHELP Parameters screen

shows CC as the P choice and None as the S choice (this is the default configuration, remember, and therefore the configuration you're likely to see) and then you decide to toggle item P to CCHELP. The program has no way of determining which of the three spooling options you want, so it does not change item S in this instance. You will even be allowed to save your choices and exit from the CCINSTAL module with Printer Assignment set to CCHELP and Initial Spool File set to None.

The program will not work properly with this combination of settings, so you must remember to select CCHELP for printing only in combination with one of the other spool file options explained next.

The Spool File Options

Press **S** for Initial Spool File to toggle through four options for this feature:

- None, the default setting, means that no spool file will be made. As explained previously, you must select None when the Printer Assignment parameter is set to CC.

- Extend CCPTR.SPL directs output intended for a printer to a guest print spool file called CCPTR.SPL.

- Print CC Ptr Output sends output to the guest printer only.

- Print/Spool - CCPTR.SPL sends output simultaneously to the guest printer and to a guest print spool file called CCPTR.SPL.

When you have made any changes you want in these CCHELP Parameters options, press **F10** to return to the main menu. Then press **X** to save the changes and exit CCINSTAL.

The spool file will be created in the working directory of the guest PC during your next connect session. You can then close the file or open a new one during a session, as is explained in Step 9.

Step 9

Changing Print Options

15

In Step 8 you learned how to configure Carbon Copy Plus for various printing and log-file options. You can also add or change these options during a connect session. Using either the CC (host) module or the CCHELP (guest) module, you press **F6** from the control screen to access the available choices. If you're using CCHELP, the screen displays the Printer/Log/DOS Control menu window shown in Figure 9.1. All but the first and last items in this window relate to printing functions.

The first item on this menu, Enter Log File Data, was introduced in Step 7. This option lets you add notes to a log file.

As you can see, this menu also lets you execute a DOS command: by using item 9, Execute a DOS Command. This option is available only on the guest PC, and the commands are

```
┌──► Your Dialogue ◄──────────────────────────────────┐
│                                                      │
│                                                      │
│  ──► Remote Operator's Dialogue ◄────────────────    │
│                                                      │
│                                                      │
├──────────────────────────┬───────────────────────── │
│  Carbon Copy (CCHELP V5.2.2)  │ PRINTER / LOG / DOS CONTROL │
│     Microcom Systems, Inc.    │ 1 -- Enter Log File Data    │
│  Licensed to:                 │ 2 -- Printer to CC          │
│  XYZ Corp.                    │ 3 -- Printer to CCHELP      │
│                               │ 4 -- Printer to Both        │
│  Data Link is Established     │ 5 -- Open a Print Spool File│
│  Printer Assigned to: CCHELP  │ 6 -- Close Current Spool File│
│  Spl File: -- NONE --         │ 7 -- Print / DeSpool Function│
│                               │ 8 -- Terminate Print Requests│
│ Time 19:16:12 │ Connect 0:04:27 │ 9 -- Execute a DOS Command │
│                               │ Select Function: _          │
│                               │                             │
│                               │  ──► Esc to Cancel ◄──      │
└──────────────────────────┴───────────────────────────┘
```

Figure 9.1: Printing choices while running CCHELP

executed only on that computer. You can't run communications software or memory-resident programs through this DOS
gateway. You type **exit** at the DOS prompt to return to the
Carbon Copy Plus session.

If you're using the CC (host) module during a session and
you press **F6**, the screen displays only the first four items on
the Printer/Log/DOS Control menu. The screen does not display the other items because, as mentioned in Step 8, the CC
module has no spool-file capabilities.

When either the host or guest operator presses **F6** to display
the printing options and then the operator of the other computer also presses **F6**, Carbon Copy Plus denies the second
operator access to the printing menu and displays the message *Please wait. Other user is busy.*

Here is how to use the printing and spooling options:

1. Press **2**, Printer to CC, to direct (or redirect) the output
    from a current host application only to the host printer.

2. Press **3**, Printer to CCHELP, to direct (or redirect) the
    output only to the guest printer.

3. Press **4**, Printer to Both, to direct the output to both
    host and guest printers.

4. Press **5**, Open a Print Spool File (on the guest computer
    only), to open an existing spool file, change from one
    spool file to another, or create a new spool file. Fig-
    ure 9.2 shows the windows that appear when you select
    this option. The window on the left lists any existing
    spool files (they bear the extension .SPL); if you want
    to activate one of these, highlight the file name and
    press **Enter**. The window on the right is where you
    enter a file name if you want to create a new spool file.

    •   If you select an existing spool file name, the screen
        displays the message *Spool File Already Exists.*

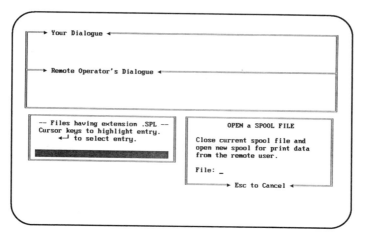

Figure 9.2: Opening a spool file

> *Should file be overwritten or extended?* Press **O** to overwrite if you want to create a new file with the same name as the old one. Press **X** if you want to add new data to be spooled to the end of the existing file.

- If you enter a file name for a new spool file, enter a maximum of eight characters, following the usual DOS rules for characters permitted in file names. Don't type an extension, because the program adds the extension .SPL automatically. Press **Enter**.

- If an existing spool file is already running when you either select or create another spool file, the screen displays the message *Spool file has been activated. Should the previous spool file be printed (Yes or No)?* Press **N** to close the old file and save it to disk for printing later. Press **Y** to print the file now to the current printer selection (host, guest, or both).

5. Press **6**, Close Current Spool File (on the guest computer only), to close the current spool file without

opening another. You'll be asked if you want to print
the file before it's closed. Press **Y** to send the data
to the current printer selection, or **N** to close the file
without printing it.

Any time your computer is functioning as a guest and a spool
file is being printed, you must close that file before you return
to the application on the host computer.

6. Press **7**, Print/DeSpool Function (on the guest com-
    puter only), to print (or despool) any existing spool file
    on the printer at the guest site. The left window dis-
    plays a list of all spool files (with the extension .SPL).
    Highlight the one you want to print and press **Enter**. If
    you want to preempt any spool file currently being
    printed and have all subsequent output from the host
    computer in the current session printed on line to the
    guest printer, type an asterisk (*****) in the right window.
    If you select this alternative, no new spool file will be
    made. Figure 9.3 shows the Print/DeSpool windows.

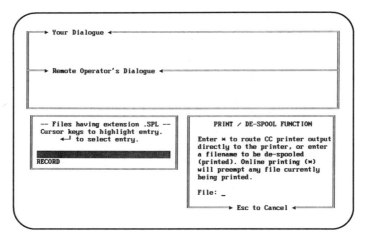

Figure 9.3: The Print/DeSpool windows

7. Press **8**, Terminate Print Requests (on the guest computer only), to stop all printing, whether spool file de-
   spooling or on-line printing. Press **Y** to confirm this
   action or **N** if you change your mind, as shown in Figure 9.4. If you cancel the printing of a spool file, the
   next time you issue a command to print this file, printing starts from the beginning of the file.

8. When you finish selecting a printer option, the program
   returns you to the main menu. Press **F10** to return to
   the application currently running on the host.

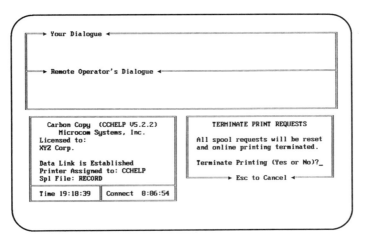

Figure 9.4: Terminating all printing

Step 10

Transferring Files

One of the most powerful features of Carbon Copy Plus is its ability to let you sit at your own computer and install and configure software on another computer at a remote location that may be hundreds or thousands of miles away. After you've completed the installation, you can even check your work by printing sample files on your own printer, using the techniques discussed in Steps 8 and 9.

The installation capability is made possible by a feature called CCDOS. CCDOS consists of a group of commands that are very similar to those in the DOS operating system and which are available only when you're using the CCHELP module of the program.

In addition to installing software, you can use CCDOS to perform other tasks, such as erasing files or transferring the contents of a directory on the host computer to a directory on your own computer. You access CCDOS by pressing **F5** to select File Transfer Package from the control screen main menu.

You won't see the **F5** menu item if you're operating a host computer, because this option is not available to the operators of computers serving as hosts. You won't see the option on the screen of a guest computer either until you've connected with a host computer, and you won't even see it then if you've accessed a host with a password that doesn't permit file transfer activities. (This restricted password category is called No CCDOS; see Step 5, where password tables are explained.)

If you're using a password with full CCDOS privileges, you can transfer files, erase them, rename them, or overwrite them. If your password has Limited CCDOS privileges, you can transfer files only to or from the host directory that is active when a session connection is made, and you can't erase or rename files.

As soon as the operator of a guest computer presses **F5**, a message appears in the lower-right window of the host menu screen stating, *File transfer is active.* From this point on, the guest and host screens are no longer linked. The screens will remain unlinked until the CCDOS session has been completed. The host will be kept informed of file transfer activities by messages displayed in the Remote Operator's Dialogue window: for instance, by the message *Writing file:* followed by the file name. The host screen will also display a bar that indicates the percentage of the current file transfer that has been completed.

The screen of the guest monitor will display the commands typed; error messages, if syntax is wrong or if errors occur in transmission; and a file-transfer progress display that shows a series of bars, one for each file transferred.

Unless background transfer (see Step 12) is being used, the host computer is disabled for any normal operation until the CCDOS operation has been completed.

The main difference between CCDOS commands and DOS operating system commands is that CCDOS uses the letter *L* to represent the guest computer and *H* to represent the host.

Transferring an Application to a Host

The following sequence demonstrates how to set up a new application on a host computer. This example uses the More-Fonts program from MicroLogic Software (Emeryville, California), a utility that generates custom soft fonts from outlines.

1. Follow the program's instruction manual to install the program in a directory on the same logical drive on the guest computer that you intend to use on the host. Some programs will not work properly if they're copied, for example, from drive C to drive D. In this example, we'll install MoreFonts on drive D of the guest computer in a directory called MOREFONT, because the intended destination is drive D of the host.

2. Log on to the guest computer directory that contains Carbon Copy Plus. Type **CCHELP** and then press **Enter** to load the CCHELP module.

3. Press **F1** and type the phone number of the host, typing the password when requested. Alternatively, you can connect to the host automatically by selecting that computer from your call table.

4. Press **Alt-RightShift** to display the connect-session control screen. Then press **F5** from the main menu to access the File Transfer Package. When the screen shown in Figure 10.1 appears, you must start using

```
                Carbon Copy (CCDOS) -- Version 5.2.2

        (Communicating with Version 3.8 or Later of Carbon Copy)

CCDOS, Carbon Copy's file transfer package, provides DOS commands to
move data files between your system (your Local PC) and the other system
(the Host PC). The major difference is that the drive specifier must
be preceded by an H for Host or L for Local. For example:

        COPY LC:TEST.DOC HC:

copies the file TEST.DOC from your system to the Host system.  CCDOS
supports full DOS pathing and wildcards.

Type HELP for more information.

Local-C:\CCPLUS>_
```

Figure 10.1: Introductory screen of the file transfer module

CCDOS commands. Note that, instead of a DOS prompt, a CCDOS prompt appears. At first, this prompt will start with the word *Local* to indicate that you can issue commands that will take effect on your own (the guest) computer.

5. Type **HD:** and press **Enter** to change the active host drive to D.

6. Type **MD HD:\MOREFONT** and press **Enter** to create a new directory, called MOREFONT, on the host.

7. Type **CD HD:\MOREFONT** and press **Enter** to change the active directory on the host to the new MOREFONT directory on the host computer D drive.

8. Type **COPY LD:\MOREFONT*.* HD:** and press **Enter** to copy the entire contents of the MOREFONT directory from the guest (or local) computer to the active directory on the host, which, at this point, is MOREFONT. Carbon Copy Plus will now use a proprietary protocol that includes data compression to transfer the files between computers at maximum speed. On the guest you'll see a screen similar to the one in Figure 10.2. When the transfer has been completed, a CCDOS prompt beginning with the word *Host* will appear, as shown in Figure 10.3. The prompt indicates that the active directory is MOREFONT.

9. Type either **EXIT** or **BYE** and press **Enter** to leave the CCDOS module and return to normal Carbon Copy Plus functions. You can now run the MoreFonts application on the host to test the installation and produce sample printouts from the application on the guest printer.

10. Terminate the connect session and remove the temporary MOREFONT directory and its contents from the hard disk of the guest PC.

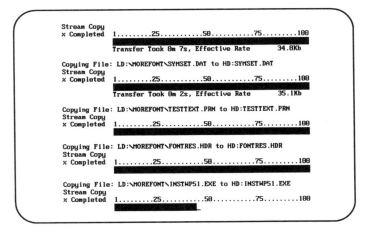

Figure 10.2: File transfer in progress, as seen by the guest

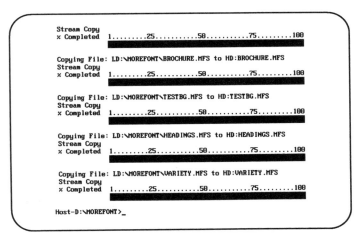

Figure 10.3: The CCDOS prompt after file transfer is complete

You can press **Ctrl-Break** at any time during a CCDOS session to abort the current command. This action affects only the current activity ; it does not return you to DOS, take you out of the CCDOS module, or terminate the connect session.

You can automate file transfers in Carbon Copy Plus by creating CCDOS batch files. This feature is handy if you need to perform the same task frequently, such as copying a weekly report from a host computer to your guest PC or installing the same software update on several host computers in your system.

You can start CCDOS batch files only from the CCDOS module, and these batch files must contain only CCDOS commands. Similar commands from the DOS operating system cannot be used.

Creating a Typical CCDOS Batch File

You can write a CCDOS batch file with the DOS EDLIN utility or any word processor that can produce a straight ASCII text file, with no embedded formatting commands. For example, you can use WordStar, creating a "nondocument" file. The batch file name can have a maximum of eight characters, plus the obligatory extension .BAT. This file name must be in the current guest directory when you issue the command to run the batch file. To start a batch file, you simply type its name, without the .BAT extension, from the CCDOS prompt and press **Enter**.

To see how the procedure works, suppose that, instead of installing the MoreFonts application on a host computer for the first time—the example used in Step 10—you want to install a new version of MoreFonts, using a batch file. In addition, you want to install an update of a menu file that shows how to access all programs installed on the host and displays the new MoreFonts version number. You want to save the previous menu file for reference. You also want to preserve a

MoreFonts font-set file, which the host operator named VARIETY.MFS, from the old version for future use. This file contains the operator's specifications for a custom font set that uses various special effects featured in the font program. At this point the Alert command sounds a beep to let you know that the copy operation is complete. Finally, you want to display a directory listing of the completed installation to be sure that all of the files were copied properly. Then you want to disconnect from the host and terminate your Carbon Copy Plus session.

The following batch file performs all of these operations.

```
HC:
CD\
REN HC:\MENU. HC:\MENU.BAK
COPY LC:\MENU. HC:
HD:
CD\
COPY HD:\MOREFONT\VARIETY.MFS HD:
CD HD:\MOREFONT
DELNV *.*
COPY HD:\VARIETY.MFS HD:
DELNV HD:\VARIETY.MFS
COPY LD:\MOREFONT\*.* HD:
ALERT
DIR
EXITP
```

Line-by-Line Explanation of Batch File

Here is a line-by-line explanation of this CCDOS batch file. Each program line from the batch file is printed separately, followed by an explanation of that line.

```
HC:
```

This first command makes drive C of the host computer the current drive.

    CD\

This Change Directory command ensures that the current directory of the host computer is the root directory.

    REN HC:\MENU. HC:\MENU.BAK

This Rename command changes the name of the MENU file in the root directory of host drive C to MENU.BAK.

Note that, with CCDOS commands, when you type the name of a file that does not have an extension, you must add a period after the file name. Thus, you enter **MENU.** as the name of the MENU file.

    COPY LC:\MENU. HC:

This Copy command copies the updated version of the MENU file from the root directory of the guest (local) computer to drive C of the host. The file is copied into the current host directory (which, in this case, is also the root).

    HD:

This command changes the active drive to host drive D.

    CD\

This Change Directory command ensures that the current directory on host drive D is the root.

    COPY HD:\MOREFONT\VARIETY.MFS HD:

This Copy command copies the MoreFonts font-set file VARIETY.MFS from the MOREFONT directory on drive D of the host computer into the current directory on drive D, which again is the root.

    CD HD:\MOREFONT

This Change Directory command changes the active directory to MOREFONT on drive D of the host.

    DELNV *.*

This Delete command deletes the entire contents of the current directory, which is now D:\MOREFONT on the host. The NV (no verification) qualifier added to the DEL command tells the program not to ask for verification before erasing the files, an important instruction when you want to run an automatic batch file. The purpose of the Delete command in this instance is to remove the old version of MoreFonts.

    COPY HD:\VARIETY.MFS HD:

This Copy command copies the file VARIETY.MFS, which was copied to the host drive D root directory to preserve it, from the root into the current directory, MOREFONT.

    DELNV HD:\VARIETY.MFS

This second Delete command deletes the temporary copy of VARIETY.MFS from the root directory of host drive D, again with no verification.

    COPY LD:\MOREFONT*.* HD:

This Copy command copies the entire contents of the MORE-FONT directory on drive D of the guest computer into the current directory (MOREFONT) of the host. This Copy command installs the new version of MoreFonts onto the host computer.

    ALERT

This command sounds an alarm on the guest computer to let the operator know that the file copying process has been completed.

DIR

This Directory command lists the contents of the current directory (D:\MOREFONT on the host computer) so you can verify that all files were copied correctly. This directory listing will scroll by too quickly to be readable during the actual connect session. It is intended for reading in the log file made of the session (as explained in Step 7). You could add the qualifier **/P** to make the display pause after each screenful of data, but the batch file would then require operator intervention to display each successive screen. Another alternate version of this command is **DIR/W**, which displays the contents of the directory in wide format.

EXITP

This command exits from the CCDOS module, ends the connect session with the host, and exits from Carbon Copy Plus. Alternate commands you could use are **EXIT**, which exits from CCDOS, preserves the connection, and returns to the control screen main menu; **EXITA**, which exits from CCDOS, preserves the connection, and returns to the application that was previously running on the host; and **EXITD**, which exits from CCDOS, disconnects from the host, and returns to the control screen main menu.

Background File Transfers

While a normal CCDOS file transfer is taking place in Carbon Copy Plus, the operator of the host PC has no control over the computer at all. The host keyboard won't function until the operator of the guest computer has completed the transfer. However, the program also gives you the option of performing file transfers in the background, meaning that the host computer can simultaneously be used for other work.

You can accomplish background file transfers in two ways: by issuing CCDOS commands one at a time or by invoking an automatic batch file. You'll learn about both methods in this Step.

Background file transfers can be initiated and controlled only from a computer functioning as a guest. The guest must have full CCDOS access privileges.

Making Background Transfers through Manual Commands

When you haven't created a batch file to automate background transfers, here's how to make those transfers manually, command by command:

1. Start CCHELP in the usual way. Then press **F1**, the Call CC User option.

2. Type the telephone number for the host PC you want to call and press **Enter**. The program will dial the number and make contact with the host.

3. When you're prompted for a password, type the password you normally use for full CCDOS access to that host. Then press **Ctrl-Enter** (not **Enter** alone).

4. You can now type any CCDOS commands that you normally use for file transfers. However, the transfers will take place in the background; the host operator retains full control of the host computer.

5. Type **EXIT** and press **Enter** when you've finished transferring files. Your CCDOS session will be terminated, and you will be disconnected from the host computer and returned to the CCHELP control screen.

Making Automatic Background Transfers

To transfer files automatically, you create a CCDOS batch file for that purpose, using the techniques you learned in Steps 11 and 12. Then you access your call table and link the batch file to a password for the host by placing a colon between the two elements, like this: PASSWORD:FILENAME. For background transfers, the combination of the password, the colon, and the batch-file name must not exceed a total of 16 characters and must include no spaces.

Follow this procedure:

1. Create the batch file. Name and save it. Like all DOS file names, the batch-file name must not exceed eight characters, not counting the extension, which must be .BAT.

2. Enter the CCINSTAL module and select item 3, Call Table.

3. Move the cursor to the line that contains the phone number and password for the host PC you want to call. (If there is no entry as yet for this host, type an identifying name for the host in column 1 and the phone number in column 2.)

4. Move the cursor to the Password column (column 3). Type the proper password for Full CCDOS privileges

on the host; or, if this column already contains the password, move the cursor to the end of the password.

5. Type a colon and then the name of the file transfer batch file you want to run automatically. Once you've typed a total of 16 characters in this column—counting the password, the colon, and the file name—you will see this warning message appear at the bottom of the screen if you try to type a seventeenth character: *No More Room In Field; Press Any Key to Continue.*

6. Press **Enter** to complete the entry and leave the line.

7. Press **F10** to return to the main System Parameters menu of CCINSTAL and then **X** to save your changes and exit from the module.

8. Enter the CCHELP module and press **F1** for Call CC User.

9. Select the name of the host from the call table window by highlighting it and pressing **Enter**.

(Instead of performing the operations in items 8 and 9, from the DOS prompt you can simply type **CCHELP**, a space, and the name of the host as shown on the call table. Then press **Enter**.)

Carbon Copy Plus will now dial the host PC, present the password automatically, and start running the batch file, which will perform the background file transfers specified. The operator of the host can continue to use that computer for other work.

If you ended your CCDOS batch file with the Exit command, you will automatically be disconnected from the host when the transfers are completed. Otherwise, you will still be in the CCDOS module and will have to type **EXIT** and press **Enter** to disconnect from the host and return to the CCHELP control screen.

Figure 12.1 shows how to add a batch-file name to the password PEACHTREE to effect background file transfer. This batch file is named REPORT, and it might be used to transfer a regular weekly report from the host PC to the guest. The combination PEACHTREE:REPORT adds up to exactly 16 characters, so you cannot add another character to the batch-file name. If you try to do so, you will see the warning message shown at the bottom of the screen.

```
╔═══════════════════════ CALL TABLE ═══════════════════════╗
║ UsT Arrow Keys, Pg Up, Pg Dn, Home & End to Position Field Pointer
║ To Edit a Field enter a character, Ins, Del or F1
║                            FUNCTION KEYS
║        F1 -- Edit Current Field            F2 -- Insert Line
║        F3 -- Delete Current Line Entry     F4 -- Sort Entries by Name
║        F5 -- Edit Current Line Emulation Table
║        F6 -- Special Phone Characters      F7 -- Print Call Table
║        F9 -- Help                          F10 - Exit to Main Menu
║ ──────────────────────────────────────────────────────────────────
║  Name              │ Telephone Number    │ Password(:Batch File)
║ ───────────────────┼─────────────────────┼──────────────────────
║  ATLANTA_OFFICE     │ 1-404-111-2222      │ PEACHTREE:REPORT
║  CHICAGO_OFFICE     │ 1-312-123-4567      │ MARINA
║
║
║
║
║ ──────────────────────────────────────────────────────────────────
║  No More Room In Field; Press Any Key to Continue_
╚════════════════════════════════════════════════════════════════════╝
```

Figure 12.1: Adding a batch-file name to the call table

Carbon Copy Plus is, in effect, two programs in one. So far you've learned about its various features that you can use in controlling a remote personal computer from your own PC. However, Carbon Copy Plus can also function as a terminal emulator. In this mode, you can use it to contact a mainframe or minicomputer. Your keyboard and screen will behave just as if they were elements of a terminal attached to the larger computer.

Your PC can emulate a DEC VT-100, except for producing double-height and double-width characters (because of the limitations of PC screens). It can also emulate the DEC VT-52, the TeleVideo TVI-920, and the IBM 3101. You can even specify the extent of the emulation, setting your PC not to respond to certain terminal commands.

When you use the program for terminal emulation, you need only one copy of Carbon Copy Plus, instead of the minimum of two copies with different serial numbers required for PC remote-control operations.

Using the Terminal Emulation Setup Menu

You don't need to perform any special installation of the terminal emulation feature. Once you've installed the program for remote use, as explained in earlier Steps, terminal emulation is available too. The general installation settings you've already established, such as the serial port to use and the type of modem, apply to terminal emulation as well.

You can reach the terminal emulation setup menu in two ways

However, you must configure the terminal emulation module so its specific settings will be appropriate for the larger computer you want to contact. You do this by using the terminal emulation setup menu, accessible either from the main CCHELP control screen menu or from the call table.

Follow this procedure to establish terminal emulation settings from the CCHELP main menu:

1. Load the CCHELP module from your CCPLUS directory or the working copy of your program disk.

2. From the main menu of the control screen, press **F7** to select Terminal Emulation. This action displays the terminal screen used to communicate with mainframes and minicomputers. The screen will be blank, except for a line at the bottom offering two items of information: The screen tells you to press **Alt-M** to display a menu, and it informs you that your computer is currently off line.

3. Press **Alt-M**. You'll see the Terminal Emulator Command menu shown in Figure 13.1.

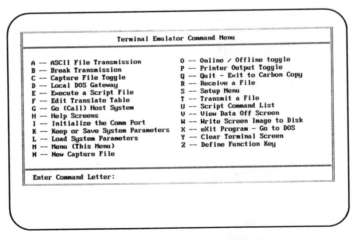

```
                    Terminal Emulator Command Menu

    A -- ASCII File Transmission        O -- Online / Offline toggle
    B -- Break Transmission             P -- Printer Output Toggle
    C -- Capture File Toggle            Q -- Quit - Exit to Carbon Copy
    D -- Local DOS Gateway              R -- Receive a File
    E -- Execute a Script File          S -- Setup Menu
    F -- Edit Translate Table           T -- Transmit a File
    G -- Go (Call) Host System          U -- Script Command List
    H -- Help Screens                   V -- View Data Off Screen
    I -- Initialize the Comm Port       W -- Write Screen Image to Disk
    K -- Keep or Save System Parameters X -- eXit Program - Go to DOS
    L -- Load System Parameters         Y -- Clear Terminal Screen
    M -- Menu (This Menu)               Z -- Define Function Key
    N -- New Capture File


  Enter Command Letter:
```

Figure 13.1: The Terminal Emulator Command menu

4. From this menu, press **S** to access the Terminal Emulator Configuration menu displayed in Figure 13.2.

5. Change any default specifications necessary by pressing the letter that represents the option. Each time you press the letter, you'll see a different choice available for the option. Toggle through the choices until you reach the one you want.

6. Press **Enter** to save your changes and leave the set-up menu, or press **Esc** to exit without saving your changes.

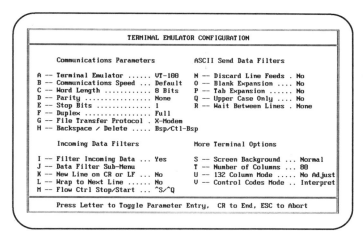

```
                    TERMINAL EMULATOR CONFIGURATION

        Communications Parameters          ASCII Send Data Filters

 A -- Terminal Emulator ...... VT-100    N -- Discard Line Feeds . No
 B -- Communications Speed ... Default   O -- Blank Expansion .... No
 C -- Word Length ........... 8 Bits     P -- Tab Expansion ...... No
 D -- Parity ................ None       Q -- Upper Case Only .... No
 E -- Stop Bits ............. 1          R -- Wait Between Lines . None
 F -- Duplex ................ Full
 G -- File Transfer Protocol . X-Modem
 H -- Backspace / Delete ..... Bsp/Ctl-Bsp

        Incoming Data Filters              More Terminal Options

 I -- Filter Incoming Data ... Yes       S -- Screen Background ... Normal
 J -- Data Filter Sub-Menu               T -- Number of Columns ... 80
 K -- New Line on CR or LF ... No        U -- 132 Column Mode ..... No Adjust
 L -- Wrap to Next Line ...... No        V -- Control Codes Mode .. Interpret
 M -- Flow Ctrl Stop/Start ... ^S/^Q

        Press Letter to Toggle Parameter Entry,  CR to End, ESC to Abort
```

Figure 13.2: The Terminal Emulator Configuration menu

Choosing Communications Parameters

Options A through H on the Terminal Emulator Configuration menu set the basic communications parameters. Here's what they mean:

• **A—Terminal Emulator**. You have six choices of terminal emulator: VT-100 (the default selection), VT-52, TVI-920, IBM 3101, Debug, and None.

The first four choices provide emulation for the terminal types listed. By changing related setup options, you can customize any of these four emulations to emulate some terminal not listed. Selecting an emulation changes the codes that are sent to the host computer when you press certain keys on your keyboard. Selecting an emulation also may cause commands sent to your computer from the host to produce special effects on your screen. The Debug option does not provide terminal emulation. Instead, it causes control codes sent from the host to be displayed unchanged on your screen, for debugging purposes, in 80-column width.

The None option causes your PC to ignore escape sequences such as Escape M sent by the host and to recognize only fundamental incoming control codes such as those for carriage returns and line feeds.

- **B—Communications Speed**. The communications speed options are Default, 110, 300, 1200, 2400, 4800, 9600, 19.2K, and 38.4K bits per second (bps). The Default setting is whatever speed you've already established in CCINSTAL. Choose a speed that will be compatible with both your equipment and the host computer.

- **C—Word Length**. You can set the word length, or the number of bits required to represent a character. You can choose 8 bits, the length normally used if parity is set to none, or 7 bits, the preferred setting if you're using odd or even parity.

- **D—Parity**. The parity choices are None, Odd, and Even. Parity is a bit added to a character as it is transmitted. The receiving system uses this bit to detect transmission errors in the character.

- **E—Stop Bits**. The stop bits setting must match that of the host computer. The default setting is 1. This setting is used with most communications speeds. The other option, 2, is normally used only when the communication speed is 110 bps. Stop bits are bits added at the end of a data character for synchronization and error detection purposes.

- **F—Duplex.** Your display choices are Full and Half. With Half Duplex selected, the terminal emulator displays each of your keystrokes on your screen as you type them for transmission to the host; the host does not echo the characters you type. With Full Duplex selected, the terminal emulator provides no display of your keystrokes; you will see the characters you type as they're echoed back to your PC from the host.

- **G—File Transfer Protocol.** You can select from six file transfer protocols: X-Modem, X-Modem Batch, Y-Modem, Y-Modem Batch, Kermit Text, and Kermit Binary. These are public-domain file transfer protocols used to provide error-free communications. Of course, you must select a protocol supported by the host computer. The Batch options allow you to issue commands for group file transfers, rather than transferring one file at a time.

- **H—Backspace / Delete.** You have two backspace choices: Bsp/Ctl-Bsp (the default setting) and Ctl-Bsp/Bsp. This option controls the operation of the **Backspace** key. Normally, in terminal emulation mode, you press your **Backspace** key by itself to obtain a normal backspace function, and you hold down the **Ctrl** key and press **Backspace** to emulate the PC **Delete** key. However, in DEC environments, the **Delete** key is used more often than **Backspace**. Therefore, for convenience, you might want to select the second option, Ctl-Bsp/Bsp. In this case, when you press the **Backspace** key by itself, it will operate like the **Delete** key; you press **Ctrl-Backspace** to obtain the backspace function.

As mentioned earlier, press **Enter** to save your selections and leave the setup menu. Press **Esc** to exit without saving your changes.

If you're not sure what communications parameters you should be using, ask the operator of the host computer to provide you with the required settings.

After setting these basic communications parameters, you should be able to communicate with most mainframes and minicomputers.

If you call other PCs as well as mainframes or minicomputers, or if you need to call two mainframes that require different terminal emulation settings, you certainly don't want to reconfigure your copy of Carbon Copy Plus every time you have to switch between these remote computer options.

Fortunately, you can make entries in your call table that will automatically provide any special communications settings required for each host computer you contact.

You accomplish this magic by accessing the terminal emulation setup menu—the Terminal Emulator Configuration menu—from the call table instead of from the CCHELP control screen.

Adding Terminal
Emulations to Your Call Table

These are the actions you take to add terminal emulation information to your call table:

1. Start the CCINSTAL module from the DOS prompt.

2. Press **3** to select the Call Table option.

3. On the call table screen, move the cursor to the line that contains an existing entry you want to modify, or move the cursor to a blank line and make a new entry, typing a name to identify the host in the first column and the phone number in the second column.

4. With the cursor still on that line, press **F5** to select Edit Current Line Emulation Table. You will immediately be switched to the Terminal Emulator Configuration screen explained in Step 13.

5. Select the emulation options you want for the host you'll be calling.

6. Press **X** to save your configuration and return to the call table.

7. Press **F10** to exit to the main CCINSTAL System Parameters menu and then press **X** to save your changes and exit to DOS.

Figure 14.1 shows a call table after the completion of this sequence. Note that the entry in the Password column has automatically changed to Emulator_Entry. This entry indicates that Carbon Copy PLUS uses specific terminal emulation parameters when calls are made to the host listed on this line of the table.

Placing a Call with Terminal Emulation

Here is how you place a call using a call table entry with a stored terminal emulation setup:

1. Enter the CCHELP module and press **F7** for Terminal Emulation. You will see the blank terminal screen.

2. Press **Alt-G** to place a call. The Call Table and Call Remote System windows associated with the CCHELP control screen will appear superimposed on the terminal screen (see Figure 14.2).

3. Use the cursor-control keys to select the name of the host you want to call from the call table. Then press **Enter**. The window on the right will show that the number is being dialed. After the connection has been made, the bottom line of the terminal screen will announce that you're on line. The output of the mainframe or minicomputer host will now appear just as it would on the screen of a real terminal for that computer.

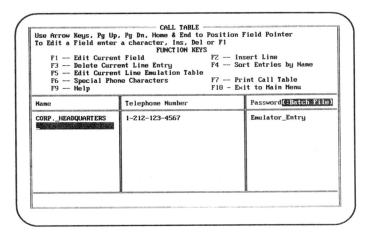

Figure 14.1: Storing a terminal emulation setup

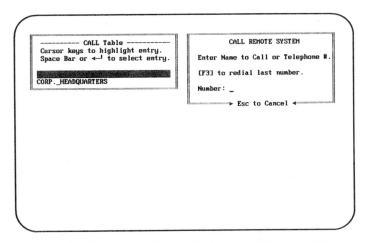

Figure 14.2: Windows on the terminal screen before a call is made

4. Follow the instructions or sign-on procedure, including password identification, required by the host computer.

5. To terminate the session, press **Alt-O**.

Step 15

Issuing Mainframe Commands

 15

When you're connected to a mainframe or minicomputer through the Carbon Copy Plus terminal emulation feature, you can use the Terminal Emulation Command menu to transmit and receive files, write a screen image to disk, and perform many other functions. You passed through this menu very briefly in Step 13, on your way to the Terminal Emulator Configuration menu.

You display the command menu by pressing **Alt-M** from the terminal screen.

In this Step you'll become familiar with several useful commands on the menu. Once you've memorized the letter associated with a command you use frequently, you can add the **Alt** key to issue the same command directly from the terminal screen. For example, you select the option Receive a File from the command menu by pressing the letter **R**. You can also select the same command from the terminal screen by pressing **Alt-R**.

Here is a list of popular options on the command menu:

- **A—ASCII File Transmission.** You can press **A** to send an ASCII text file to the host computer. You'll be prompted for the file name. If the file isn't in your current directory, you must type the drive letter and complete path so Carbon Copy Plus can find the file. Then press **Enter** to start the data transfer. No error correction will be provided during transmission. You must use a different option, T—Transmit a File, if you want to transmit ASCII files with error correction.

- **B—Break Transmission.** When you press **B**, you simply send a BREAK signal to the host. Large computers sometimes require this signal to interrupt a program.

- **C—Capture File Toggle.** This option can capture all keystrokes sent to and from the host computer in an ASCII file so you'll have a record of your session. The option is a toggle command, so pressing **C** will have different results, depending on the status of your PC. If you don't have a capture file open, you'll be prompted for a file name to start one; if you don't provide a file extension, the extension .DAT will be added automatically. If a capture file is already open, pressing **C** will suspend data capture to the file temporarily. If the file is open and suspended, you press **C** to resume the capture of data. You can view .DAT files by using the DOS TYPE command. See also the N—New Capture File option.

- **D—Local DOS Gateway.** This option lets you leave the terminal emulator temporarily to issue DOS commands without breaking your connection with the host computer. As soon as you press **D**, you'll see the DOS prompt. This option is handy for quickly preparing a file to send to the host or for formatting a disk you'll need for storing a file you're about to receive. Type **EXIT** and press **Enter** to return to the terminal emulator. Remember that when you exit temporarily to DOS, your phone line is still in use, and any long distance charges will still be accumulating.

- **G—Go (Call) Host System.** This is the same command introduced in Step 14 as **Alt-G,** to call a host from the terminal screen. When you want to call a host from the command menu, you press **G** alone. As with all other commands issued directly from this menu, you press the letter without the **Alt** key.

- **H—Help Screens.** You press **H** to display a help screen that shows how your keyboard has been remapped to emulate the terminal you've selected. For example, as Figure 15.1 shows, when you're using

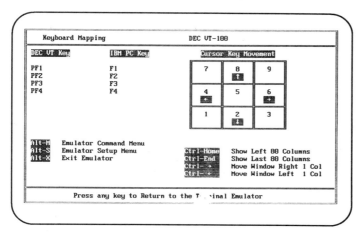

Figure 15.1: The DEC VT-100 help screen

DEC VT-100 emulation, you press **F1** on your PC to
represent the DEC VT key **PF1**.

- **N—New Capture File.** You use this command to
  switch from one capture file to another. The C—Capture File Toggle command explained earlier opens a
  new capture file or suspends or restarts a current file.
  When you use the **N** option and follow the prompt to
  provide a name for a capture file, the program automatically closes any previous capture file already running. To append data to an existing capture file, you
  type /A after a file name.

- **O—Online/Offline Toggle.** You can press **O** during a
  terminal emulation session to go to local operation
  temporarily from the current online or offline status of
  your terminal screen. When you switch to local operation, what you type goes only to your own screen. This
  mode is useful for editing text displayed on the screen
  and then saving it to disk with the W—Write Screen
  Image to Disk command. After you've finished with

your local activities, press **O** again to resume the previous online or offline status. While you're in local
mode, a buffer will capture any data transmitted by
the host computer and will display the data when you
return online—unless you've disabled the buffer feature on the setup menu by setting the flow control
option (item M) to None.

- **P—Printer Output Toggle.** Press **P** to send all of the
dialog between your PC and the host computer to your
printer as well as to display the dialog on your terminal
screen. Press **P** again to stop sending the output to the
printer.

- **Q—Quit - Exit to Carbon Copy.** This option closes
the terminal emulator and returns you to the Carbon
Copy Plus control screen. If you issue this command
during a connect session, you'll also be disconnected
from the host.

- **R—Receive a File.** This option sets up your PC to receive a file or group of files from the host computer
using the file transfer protocol you selected in the setup
menu. You'll be prompted to provide the name of the
file in which to store the data. To append the data to an
existing file, add /A to the file name.

- **S—Setup Menu** This option takes you to the setup
menu introduced in Step 13.

- **T—Transmit a File.** Use this option to send a file to
the host computer. You'll be prompted for a file name.
The program will use the file transfer protocol that you
established in the setup menu.

- **V—View Data Off Screen.** If the number of columns
for your screen is set to 80—the default value in the
setup menu—you can press **V** to see data that has
scrolled off the screen. You can use the **Up** and **Down
Arrow** keys to scroll forward or backward a line at a
time. Use **PgUp** and **PgDn** to scroll a page at a time.

Press **Home** to see the earliest line of data entered and press **End** to see the most recent line. Press **Esc** to return to normal terminal screen operation. Unless you've disabled the buffer from the setup menu, you'll then see any data that was sent from the host computer while you were viewing the data previously transmitted.

- **W—Write Screen Image to Disk**. Press **W** if you want to save what's currently displayed on screen to an ASCII disk file. You'll be prompted for a file name.

- **X—eXit Program - Go to DOS**. Press **X** to disconnect from the host computer (if you're in a session), exit from the terminal emulator and from Carbon Copy Plus, and return to DOS. Think twice before you issue this command, because it abruptly "pulls the plug" on all of your current Carbon Copy Plus activities.

- **Y—Clear Terminal Screen**. This option is purely a housekeeping function. It erases all data from your terminal screen. You might want to issue this command in order to have a clean screen for the capture of data to be transmitted from the host computer.

With the commands explained in this Step, you can perform the most common tasks in a terminal emulation session.

Changing the Screen Display

You can change several attributes of your screen display. Some of these options can help you communicate with certain host computers. Carbon Copy Plus provides four attributes that you can change from the Terminal Emulator Configuration menu: Screen Background, Number of Columns, 132 Column Mode, and Control Codes Mode. Access these setup menu options through the CCHELP module. (You can also reach this setup menu through CCINSTAL and the call table, as explained in Step 14, if your goal is to change the attributes only for a particular host listed in the call table.)

Changing Display
Options on the Setup Menu

The following section tells how to make setup menu changes and what these changes mean.

1. Load CCHELP from the DOS prompt of your Carbon Copy Plus directory or the working copy of your program disk.

2. Press **F7** for Terminal Emulation. The blank terminal screen appears.

3. Press **Alt-M** to display the Terminal Emulator Command menu; then press **S** to access the setup menu. For a shortcut to the setup menu, press **Alt-S** from the terminal screen; you'll bypass the command menu and instead go directly to the setup menu. The setup menu lists the screen display options under the heading More Terminal Options.

4. Press **S** for Screen Background if you want to change your display from its normal mode to reverse video. In reverse video, any text that previously appeared in

white lettering, for example, will now appear in black. The S command is a toggle, so if you press **S** a second time, the display will change to normal mode again. Any change takes effect as soon as you leave the set-up menu.

5. Press **T** for Number of Columns to change the width of the screen from its default setting of 80 characters on each line to 132 characters on each line. The VT-100 terminal emulation provides the capacity for a 132-column display. However, Carbon Copy PLUS cannot save data in 132-column format when the data scrolls off the screen, and you can't use the emulator's View Data Off Screen command to view this data either. The T option is another toggle. Press **T** a second time to restore the default 80-column format.

6. Press **U** for 132 Column Mode if you want the cursor to stay in view automatically when Number of Columns is set to 132. The default setting is No Adjust, meaning that you may have to scroll manually to keep the cursor in sight. When you toggle to the alternate choice, Adjust, the display will scroll automatically to accomplish this goal.

7. Press **V** for Control Codes Mode to change the way the screen displays control codes and escape sequences transmitted by the host computer. The default setting is Interpret, meaning that your screen will interpret special instructions from the host as normally intended. The purpose of the alternate option, Display, is to permit debugging activities. When you toggle to Display, the control codes and escape sequences appear on your screen as the special IBM symbols that represent the code and sequence values. After you've completed a debugging session, press **V** again to return the screen to its normal appearance.

8. When you've completed any changes you want to make in the display settings, press **Enter** to save them

or **Esc** to cancel them. In either case, you'll be returned to the terminal screen.

9. You can now press **Alt-M** to display the Terminal Emulator Command menu so you can perform other tasks or exit from the emulator. If you do you want to leave the emulator, you can press **Alt-Q** from the terminal screen to return to the Carbon Copy Plus control screen or **Alt-X** to exit to DOS.

Changing Menu Colors

The default setting on a color monitor displays text in yellow on a black background, with borders in green. However, the CCINSTAL menu also provides several other choices. Here is a list of the available choices, showing the color combinations as they appear on the CCINSTAL System Parameters screen:

- Yellow and green text, black background, green borders (default display)
- White text, blue background, yellow and red borders
- Red and white text, blue background, blue and white borders
- White text, black background, white and black borders
- Red and white text, black background, red and white borders
- Black and blue text, brown background, yellow and blue border
- Red and blue text, white background, white and blue borders
- White and black text, green background, black borders
- Magenta and white text, black background, red and white borders

- Green text, black background, black and green borders
- Cyan text, black background, red and white borders

The way the colors in the preceding groups are used will vary according to the menus or windows displayed.

You make these menu color changes like this:

1. Start CCINSTAL from the DOS prompt. This action displays the System Parameters main menu.

2. In the General Parameters section, press **F** for Menu Colors. Every time you press **F**, the menu color choice toggles to another color combination, and the System Parameters menu itself appears in the new colors.

3. When you're satisfied with the color changes, press **X** to save your changes and return to DOS, or press **Q** to exit without making any changes.

Any color changes you make here will apply to all Carbon Copy Plus menus, not just to the terminal emulator module.

Auto Calling Online Services

You can use script files in Carbon Copy Plus to automate any sequence of terminal emulator commands you would otherwise have to execute manually. These script files can be real timesavers when they automate routines that you perform regularly.

Scripts are really small programs and follow typical programming conventions. Fortunately, you don't have to be a programmer to use scripts. The principles of writing them are easy to learn. In addition, Carbon Copy Plus comes with some ready-made scripts that you may find handy.

The scripts the program provides are for logging on to mainframe computers that let you access online services such as CompuServe, Dow Jones, GEnie, the Source, Delphi, Newsnet, LEXIS, and the Official Airline Guide. The scripts are shipped on the Utility disk furnished with Carbon Copy Plus. If you have a hard disk, you probably already copied these files to your Carbon Copy Plus directory when you installed the program. If you have a floppy disk system, the files should be on the working copy of your Utility disk.

Using a Script for an Online Service

To use one of the Carbon Copy Plus scripts for an online service, follow this sequence:

1. Use the DOS DIR command to make sure that the script you want is listed in your Carbon Copy Plus directory or on the working copy of your Utility disk. These script files are identified by the name of the online service involved, and the file names end with the .CCS extension.

2. Using the DOS EDLIN utility or a word processor that can create and edit plain ASCII files, edit the script in question to eliminate features you don't want. For example, the CompuServe script includes sections for logging on through the CompuServe Network, Telenet, or Tymnet. Obviously, you would want to use only one of these sections in a single script.

3. Edit the appropriate lines in the script to include your own identification and password instead of the asterisks (***) provided to show you where to type your personal modifications.

4. Return to the DOS prompt and log on to your Carbon Copy Plus directory or Utility disk again, if necessary. Use a utility there, called CCS.EXE, to compile the script and to make it functional. Type the command **CCS**, a space, and the name of the script you want to compile, without including its .CCS extension; for example, type **CCS DOWJONES**. Press **Enter**. An executable form of the script will be created with the new extension .CCC. As the script is being compiled, CCS will inform you of any syntax errors that you might have introduced accidentally. Once the script has been successfully compiled, it's ready for use.

5. Load the CCHELP module and press **F7** to access the terminal emulator screen.

6. From the terminal emulator screen, press **Alt-E** to execute a script file (or press **E** from the Terminal Emulator Command menu).

7. Highlight the script file name you want and press **Enter**. The script will now run.

8. To abort the script at any time before it reaches its normal conclusion, press **Esc**.

Explanation of a Sample Script

The following script illustrates the programming language used in Carbon Copy Plus scripts. This script logs you on to MCI Mail through the Tymnet telephone network.

```
jump begin
label PLEASE
clear
mess PLEASE TRY AGAIN. MCI IS NOT RESPONDING.
.
bye
abort
label begin
wait delay 20
reply a|
wait string "please log in:"
reply MCIMAIL|
wait string "name:"
reply *** ID ***|
wait string "password:"
reply *** PW ***|
otimeout 100 jump PLEASE
wait string "Opened."
```

This script assumes that you dial Tymnet before you run the script, and that the call is answered. Here is an explanation of the individual lines in this script:

```
jump begin
```

The word *jump* always works in conjunction with a label. When the program encounters *jump* followed by the name of a label, it skips to the line where that label is entered. In this case, *jump* makes the program skip to line 8 of the script, which reads *label begin*. The word *label* before the word *begin* identifies *begin* as a label. A label serves as a place marker to guide the course of script execution to a particular segment of the program.

```
label PLEASE
```

The second line of the script identifies another label, *PLEASE*. In this instance, the label positions the program so that it can display a message that tells the user that MCI Mail is not responding.

```
clear
```

This command clears the screen in preparation for displaying the message to the user.

```
mess    PLEASE TRY AGAIN.  MCI IS NOT
RESPONDING.
```

Here is the actual message, preceded by the letters *mess,* for *messenge,* which indicate that the words that follow are to be displayed on the screen.

The next line of the script is a single period. A period is required to terminate all messages, because one message could consist of several lines.

```
bye
```

This command ends the call and disconnects the session.

```
abort
```

This command aborts the execution of the script and returns the terminal emulator to manual operation.

```
label begin
```

The label *begin* marks the actual beginning of the program

and the place in the script to which the first line, *jump begin,* directs execution.

```
wait delay 20
```

This line causes a 2.0-second delay to allow time for a connection to be made with Tymnet.

```
reply a|
```

A *reply* line specifies the response your computer will issue to the host. This reply transmits the letter *a* followed by a carriage return.

```
wait string "please log in:"
```

This line directs the script to wait for a message from the host (Tymnet) ending with the string "please log in:" before the script sends the next scheduled reply.

```
reply MCIMAIL|
```

This reply tells Tymnet that you want to be connected through Tymnet to MCI Mail. The reply ends with the symbol |, which represents a carriage return.

```
wait string "name:"
```

This line directs the script to wait for a prompt from MCI Mail that ends with the string ''name:''

```
reply *** ID ***|
```

This line directs your computer to reply with your MCI identification number. You must replace the string "*** ID ***" with your own MCI ID. The reply ends with a carriage return.

```
wait string "password:"
```

This line directs the script to wait for MCI Mail to transmit a prompt that ends with the string "password:"

```
reply *** PW ***
```

This line directs your computer to transmit your password to MCI Mail. You must replace the string "*** PW ***" with your MCI password. The reply ends with a carriage return.

```
otimeout 100 jump PLEASE
```

This line directs the script to wait 10.0 seconds for another transmission from MCI Mail. If nothing is received, the script skips to the label *PLEASE* earlier in the sequence, which will cause the section of the script to be executed that informs you MCI has *not* responded, hangs up the connection, and terminates script execution.

```
wait string "Opened."
```

If the expected message ending with the string "Opened" is received from MCI Mail within 10.0 seconds, this line directs the script to terminate, leaving you online with MCI Mail and ready to use the terminal screen to conduct your business with the service.

Most of the scripts provided with Carbon Copy Plus include programming alternatives. They're shipped so that each script can be compiled and used for its most common purpose as soon as you enter your personal identification and password. For example, the CompuServe script assumes that you want to log on to that service through CompuServe's own network. If you want to log on through Telenet or Tymnet, you need to use the appropriate segment included in the script. To avoid compiling and execution errors, each line of the Telenet and Tymnet segments is preceded with a semicolon (;), in effect making the line a comment line that will be ignored during script execution. To use these alternate segments, you need to extract the portion you want from the script and place it in a new file with a .CCS extension. Then use EDLIN or your word processor to remove the semicolon at the beginning of each programming line.

Running a Script Automatically

You can make a script execute automatically. Follow this sequence:

1. Start CCINSTAL.

2. Create a terminal emulator entry, as explained in Step 14.

3. From the Terminal Emulator Configuration menu, select **W** for Script File.

4. When prompted, type the name of your script file, without the extension, and press **Enter**.

5. Press **X** to return to the previous menu, **F10** to exit to the main menu, and **X** again to save your changes and leave CCINSTAL.

Thereafter, each time you call the host for which you created the terminal emulator entry, the script file will run automatically.

Filtering Incoming Data

Using Carbon Copy Plus you can filter data you receive from a host computer. You may want to do this to help your PC do a better job of emulating a certain terminal, to reduce line noise during data transmission, to improve the characteristics of transmission in other ways, or to prevent the execution of certain commands from the host.

You control the options for filtering incoming data from the Terminal Emulator Configuration menu. Here's how:

1. Start CCHELP from the DOS prompt, which will display the control screen.

2. Press **F7** for Terminal Emulation. Then press **Alt-S** to bypass the Terminal Emulator Command menu and go directly to the Terminal Emulator Configuration menu.

3. Press **I** to select the Filter Incoming Data option. The default setting for this option is Yes, meaning the data will be filtered in certain respects. The first time you press **I**, you toggle this option to No and eliminate filtering. Press **I** again to restore filtering. The default filtering setting masks the high-order bit (bit 8) from incoming data, converting ASCII codes 128 through 255 to the range 0 through 127 and thereby eliminating nontext characters that may otherwise be erroneously transmitted due to noise on the line. You may also want to mask the high-order bit to facilitate VT-100 or VT-52 emulation. The filtering also removes control codes (codes 0 through 31), according to the current settings in the Filter submenu (explained next).

4. Press **J** to display the Filter submenu. When the preceding Filter Incoming Data option is set to Yes, the settings on the Filter submenu determine which control codes from the host computer get through and which

are ignored. The Filter submenu displays 32 control characters with a plus (+) or minus (-) sign under each one. The terminal emulator responds only to control codes for which the setting is plus (+). Therefore, in the default settings shown in Figure 18.1, the only control codes accepted will be G, H, I, J, L, and M. You press the letter that represents a control code to toggle that code between plus and minus. For example, because the letter G has a plus sign under it, your PC will accept Control G codes from the host computer. For example, in DEC terminal emulation, Control G causes a bell to sound.

Figure 18.1: The Filter submenu with default settings

If you're using VT-100 or VT-52 emulation and are filtering incoming data, you must have a plus (+) sign under the Control X option, because that code is required.

5. Press **Enter** to save your Filter submenu changes and return to the setup menu, or press **Esc** to cancel any changes.

6. Press **K** for New Line on CR or LF if you want to change the default setting of No to Yes (or to change the option back to No again; it's another toggle). When this option is set to Yes, the terminal emulator both performs a carriage return and moves the cursor down one line when the program receives a command to perform either action from the host. This option lets the program work properly with those host computers that issue only carriage returns or only line feeds between lines, but not both. Issuing only carriage returns or only line feeds can cause text lines to overwrite one another on your PC or to be broken incorrectly in the middle of a line into multiple lines.

7. Press **L** to toggle the Wrap to Next Line option from its default setting of No to Yes. A Yes setting makes the terminal emulator automatically wrap lines of text received from a host computer that are longer than the width of your screen. Some hosts do send lines that are too long without providing carriage returns or line feeds; this action can cause your cursor to stop when it reaches the right edge of the screen and to lose the remaining text on the transmitted line. The Yes setting should correct this problem.

8. Press **M** to toggle Flow Ctrl Stop/Start between three options: Control S/Control Q, Control Q/Control S, and None. Choose the first option to make the terminal emulator send Control S to tell the host to stop sending data and Control Q to tell the host to resume; these codes will then be sent automatically to regulate data flow when the host is transmitting data faster than your PC can receive it. The second option is for the reverse situation, when your PC is sending data to the host faster than it can be received; the terminal emulator stops sending data when it receives a Control S from the host and resumes when it receives a Control Q. The None option provides no flow control in either direction.

Regardless of the flow-control setting, you can always manually send Control S to tell the host to stop sending data and Control Q to tell it to resume transmission.

9. Press **Enter** to save your choices or **Esc** to discard them. Either way, you'll be returned to the terminal screen.

10. Press **Alt-Q** to return to the control screen or **Alt-X** to return to DOS.

Filtering Outgoing Data

15

The Terminal Emulator Configuration menu provides several options that help make the data you send more compatible with the requirements of various host computers. These options alter only the transmitted data, not your original files—important in those situations where you may want to use the transmitted data for some additional purpose internally, such as in the preparation of a newsletter or report.

The options affect only text files sent using the A - ASCII File Transmission command on the Terminal Emulator Command menu (explained in Step 15).

The following instructions show you how to set these options and how they will affect your transmission.

1. Start CCHELP from the DOS prompt, thereby displaying the control screen.

2. Press **F7** for Terminal Emulation.

3. Press **Alt-S** to bypass the Terminal Emulator Command menu and go directly to the setup menu. These options are grouped under the subheading ASCII Send Data Filters.

4. Press **N** to toggle the Discard Line Feeds option between No and Yes (the default setting is No). When the setting is Yes, the terminal emulator discards the line feeds in text files transmitted to the host computer. Some hosts expect lines received from their terminals to end only with a carriage return.

5. Press **O** for Blank Expansion to toggle this option between No and Yes (the default setting is No). When the setting is Yes, the terminal emulator adds a space to any blank line transmitted in a text file, making the

line, in effect, not really blank. Use this option if the host computer interprets a blank line as the end of the transmission.

6. Press **P** to toggle Tab Expansion between No and Yes (the default setting is No). Use this option if the host computer doesn't handle the tab character properly. With the option set to Yes, the terminal emulator converts tab stops into the equivalent number of spaces required to emulate eight-character tabs.

7. Press **Q** to toggle Upper Case Only between No and Yes (the default setting is No). When the setting is Yes, the terminal emulator converts all lowercase letters into capital (or uppercase) letters. Some host programs cannot handle lowercase letters.

8. Press **R** for Wait Between Lines to change this option from the default setting of None to one of the following other choices: For CR, Manual, 0.1 Sec, 0.5 Sec, or 1.0 Sec. This option lets you slow down your transmission of text to the host if the terminal emulator is sending data to the host faster than that computer can process it. If you select For CR, the terminal emulator waits for the host to send a carriage return before transmitting the next line of the file. If you select Manual, the terminal emulator prompts you to press any key after it sends each line of data; in effect, this means that you tell the emulator exactly when to send each line. The other settings—0.1 Sec, 0.5 Sec, and 1.0 Sec—make the emulator wait automatically for the specified length of time between transmission of each line of text.

9. When you have completed any changes you want in these filters for outgoing ASCII text files, press **Enter** to save your changes and return to the terminal screen, or press **Esc** to discard the changes and return to the screen.

10. Press **Alt-Q** to exit from the terminal emulator and return to the Carbon Copy Plus control screen, or press **Alt-X** to exit to DOS.

Redefining Function Keys

When you're using Carbon Copy Plus on your PC to emulate a terminal for a larger computer, the functions of some keys are changed temporarily to represent keys found on that terminal. For example, an IBM 3101 terminal has a special key called DEL LINE; when you press it, a line of text is deleted. On your PC, the terminal emulator assigns the key combination Alt-F4 to represent that 3101 key function.

However, you can define or redefine any of your PC function key combinations through the Terminal Emulator Command menu. You can control 40 key combinations in all: the 10 function keys by themselves and in combination with the Shift, Ctrl, and Alt keys. Any keys you don't redefine will retain their default definitions for the emulation selected.

You can use this capability to redefine function keys in many ways. For example, you can use this capability to automate the issuance of a command sequence you use every day to start a certain program on the host computer; or you can use the capability simply to store a long name to avoid retyping it. You can even redefine a function key to create an auto-responder: a string of text that is sent automatically to the host as soon as the host transmits some specific text sequence.

Using the Function Key Definition Window

Here's how to use the function key redefinition feature:

1. Start CCHELP from the DOS prompt, which displays the control screen.

2. Press **F7** for Terminal Emulation. You'll see the blank terminal screen.

3. Press **Alt-M** to display the Terminal Emulation Command menu.

4. Press **Z** for Define Function Key. The function key definition window will appear, as shown in Figure 20.1.

5. To see what keys are currently defined, just press **Enter**. This action will display a screen similar to Figure 20.2, listing all of the key assignments for the terminal currently being emulated.

6. Press any key to return to the function key definition window.

7. To redefine a key, first indicate the key to be used. You do this by typing a number **1** through **10** to represent a function key by itself, or the number preceded by **S**, **C**, or **A** to represent a function key to be pressed in combination with the **Shift**, **Ctrl**, or **Alt** key.

8. Type the definition you want assigned to the function key. You don't need to enter a space or any other character between the key designation and the definition.

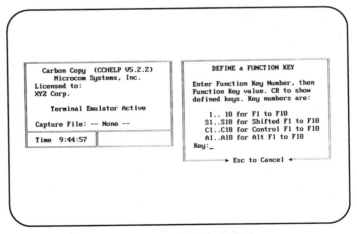

Figure 20.1: The function key definition window

You can type only as many characters as will fit into
the window (a total of 29, including the identification
of the function key and the definition).

9. Press **Enter** to save the definition or **Esc** to cancel it.

10. Each time you complete a definition, you'll be returned
to the same window, so you can enter as many definitions as you like in a single session. Press **Esc** to end
the definition session and return to the terminal screen.

11. Press **Alt-Q** to exit the emulator and return to the control screen, or press **Alt-X** to leave the Carbon Copy
Plus program and return to DOS.

Obviously, it makes sense to choose for your definition a
function key combination that is not already assigned. If you
replace an existing definition, make sure that you won't need
it when you use that terminal emulation to contact a host
computer.

```
                        ---- Function Keys ----
            F1 = +aΓ            F6 = +fΓ
            F2 = +bΓ            F7 = +gΓ
            F3 = +cΓ            F8 = +hΓ
            F4 = +dΓ            F9 =
            F5 = +eΓ            F10=
                      ---- Shifted Function Keys ----
            F1 =                F6 =
            F2 =                F7 =
            F3 =                F8 =
            F4 =                F9 =
            F5 =                F10=
                      ---- Control Function Keys ----
            F1 =                F6 =
            F2 =                F7 =
            F3 =                F8 =
            F4 =                F9 =
            F5 =                F10=
                        ---- ALT Function Keys ----
            F1 = +P             F6 = +J
            F2 = +Q             F7 = +A
            F3 = +N             F8 = +B
            F4 = +O             F9 = +D
            F5 = +I             F10= +C
                    Press Any Key to Continue
```

*Figure 20.2: Function key definitions for IBM 3101 terminal
emulation*

To remove a definition, type the function key number by itself and press **Enter**.

Using Special Symbols to Represent Control Codes

When you type definitions, you must use special symbols to represent some control codes, as follows:

For this code:	*Type this:*
Carriage return (**Enter**)		or **^M**
Escape (**Esc**)	**^[**
Line feed	**^J**
Pause (2 seconds)	~ (a tilde)

Setting Up an Auto-Responder

You can designate any of the 40 function key combinations as an auto-responder. When a function key is defined as an auto-responder, you don't press the key to use it. Instead, the terminal emulator waits until it receives a string of text you've specified in the definition from the host computer; then it transmits to the host another string of text you've also specified.

You define an auto-responder by typing the text expected from the host computer bracketed by dollar signs ($). For example, the following definition entry assigned to the Alt-F9 function key combination would cause the emulator to wait for the host to send the string "Password?" Then the emulator would respond with the password GEORGE, followed by a carriage return.

```
A9 $Password?$GEORGE|
```

An auto-responder makes no distinction between uppercase and lowercase letters transmitted from the host and ignores any spaces or control codes received. The auto-responder feature is programmed in this manner so that the emulator recognizes the text even if it arrives on separate lines.

Auto-responders become inoperative temporarily any time a script file is running.

Index

Selections from The SYBEX Library

UTILITIES

Mastering the Norton Utilities
Peter Dyson
373pp. Ref. 575-1
In-depth descriptions of each Norton utility make this book invaluable for beginning and experienced users alike. Each utility is described clearly with examples and the text is organized so that readers can put Norton to work right away. Version 4.5.

Mastering PC Tools Deluxe
Peter Dyson
400pp. Ref. 654-5
A complete hands-on guide to the timesaving—and "lifesaving"—utility programs in Version 5.5 of PC Tools Deluxe. Contains concise tutorials and in-depth discussion of every aspect of using PC Tools—from high speed backups, to data recovery, to using Desktop applications.

Mastering SideKick Plus
Gene Weisskopf
394pp. Ref. 558-1
Employ all of Sidekick's powerful and expanded features with this hands-on guide to the popular utility. Features include comprehensive and detailed coverage of time management, note taking, outlining, auto dialing, DOS file management, math, and copy-and-paste functions.

Up & Running with Norton Utilities
Rainer Bartel
140pp. Ref. 659-6
Get up and running in the shortest possible time in just 20 lessons or "steps." Learn to restore disks and files, use UnErase, edit your floppy disks, retrieve lost data and more. Or use the book to evaluate the software before you purchase. Through Version 4.2.

Up & Running with PC Tools Deluxe 6
Thomas Holste
180pp. Ref.678-2
Learn to use this software program in just 20 basic steps. Readers get a quick, inexpensive introduction to using the Tools for disaster recovery, disk and file management, and more.

COMMUNICATIONS

Mastering Crosstalk XVI (Second Edition)
Peter W. Gofton
225pp. Ref. 642-1
Introducing the communications program Crosstalk XVI for the IBM PC. As well as providing extensive examples of command and script files for programming Crosstalk, this book includes a detailed description of how to use the program's more advanced features, such as windows, talking to mini or mainframe, customizing the keyboard and answering calls and background mode.

Mastering PROCOMM PLUS
Bob Campbell
400pp. Ref. 657-X
Learn all about communications and information retrieval as you master and use PROCOMM PLUS. Topics include choosing and using a modem; automatic dialing; using on-line services (featuring CompuServe) and more. Through Version 1.1b; also covers PROCOMM, the "shareware" version.

Mastering Serial Communications
Peter W. Gofton
289pp. Ref. 180-2
The software side of communications, with details on the IBM PC's serial programming, the XMODEM and Kermit protocols, non-ASCII data transfer, interrupt-level programming and more. Sample programs in C, assembly language and BASIC.

HARDWARE

From Chips to Systems: An Introduction to Microcomputers (Second Edition)
Rodnay Zaks
Alexander Wolfe
580pp. Ref. 377-5
The best-selling introduction to microcomputer hardware—now fully updated, revised, and illustrated. Such recent advances as 32-bit processors and RISC

architecture are introduced and explained for the first time in a beginning text.

Microprocessor Interfacing Techniques (Third Edition)
Austin Lesea
Rodnay Zaks
456pp. Ref. 029-6
This handbook is for engineers and hobbyists alike, covering every aspect of interfacing microprocessors with peripheral devices. Topics include assembling a CPU, basic I/O, analog circuitry, and bus standards.

The RS-232 Solution (Second Edition)
Joe Campbell
193pp. Ref. 488-7
For anyone wanting to use their computer's serial port, this complete how-to guide is updated and expanded for trouble-free RS-232-C interfacing from scratch. Solution shows you how to connect a variety of computers, printers, and modems, and it includes details for IBM PC AT, PS/2, and Macintosh.

NETWORKS

The ABC's of Local Area Networks
Michael Dortch
212pp. Ref. 664-2
This jargon-free introduction to LANs is fur current and prospective users who see general information, comparative options, a look at the future, and tips for effective LANs use today. With comparisons of Token-Ring, PC Network, Novell, and others.

The ABC's of Novell Netware
Jeff Woodward
282pp. Ref. 614-6
For users who are new to PC's or networks, this entry-level tutorial outlines each basic element and operation of Novell. The ABC's introduces computer hardware and software, DOS, network organization and security, and printing and communicating over the netware system.

Mastering Novell Netware
Cheryl C. Currid
Craig A. Gillett
500pp. Ref. 630-8
This book is a thorough guide for System Administrators to installing and operating a microcomputer network using Novell Netware. Mastering covers actually setting up a network from start to finish, design, administration, maintenance, and troubleshooting.

Networking with TOPS
Steven William Rimmer
350pp. Ref. 565-4
A hands on guide to the most popular user friendly network available. This book will walk a user through setting up the hardware and software of a variety of TOPS configurations, from simple two station networks through whole offices. It explains the realities of sharing files between PC compatibles and Macintoshes, of sharing printers and other peripherals and, most important, of the real world performance one can expect when the network is running.

OPERATING SYSTEMS

The ABC's of DOS 4
Alan R. Miller
275pp. Ref. 583-2
This step-by-step introduction to using DOS 4 is written especially for beginners. Filled with simple examples, *The ABC's of DOS 4* covers the basics of hardware, software, disks, the system editor EDLIN, DOS commands, and more.

ABC's of MS-DOS (Second Edition)
Alan R. Miller
233pp. Ref. 493-3
This handy guide to MS-DOS is all many PC users need to manage their computer files, organize floppy and hard disks, use EDLIN, and keep their computers organized. Additional information is given about utilities like Sidekick, and there is a DOS command and program summary. The second edition is fully updated for Version 3.3.

DOS Assembly Language Programming
Alan R. Miller
365pp. 487-9
This book covers PC-DOS through 3.3, and gives clear explanations of how to assemble, link, and debug 8086, 8088, 80286, and 80386 programs. The example assembly language routines are valuable for students and programmers alike.

DOS Instant Reference
SYBEX Prompter Series

Greg Harvey
Kay Yarborough Nelson
220pp. Ref. 477-1, 4 ¾" × 8"
A complete fingertip reference for fast, easy on-line help:command summaries, syntax, usage and error messages. Organized by function—system commands, file commands, disk management, directories, batch files, I/O, networking, programming, and more. Through Version 3.3.

DOS User's Desktop Companion
SYBEX Ready Reference Series
Judd Robbins
969pp. Ref. 505-0
This comprehensive reference covers DOS commands, batch files, memory enhancements, printing, communications and more information on optimizing each user's DOS environment. Written with step-by-step instructions and plenty of examples, this volume covers all versions through 3.3.

Encyclopedia DOS
Judd Robbins
1030pp. Ref. 699-5
A comprehensive reference and user's guide to all versions of DOS through 4.0. Offers complete information on every DOS command, with all possible switches and parameters -- plus examples of effective usage. An invaluable tool.

Essential OS/2
(Second Edition)
Judd Robbins
445pp. Ref. 609-X
Written by an OS/2 expert, this is the guide to the powerful new resources of the OS/2 operating system standard edition 1.1 with presentation manager. Robbins introduces the standard edition, and details multitasking under OS/2, and the range of commands for installing, starting up, configuring, and running applications. For Version 1.1 Standard Edition.

Essential PC-DOS
(Second Edition)
Myril Clement Shaw
Susan Soltis Shaw
332pp. Ref. 413-5
An authoritative guide to PC-DOS, including version 3.2. Designed to make experts out of beginners, it explores everything from disk management to batch file programming. Includes an 85-page command summary. Through Version 3.2.

Graphics Programming
Under Windows
Brian Myers
Chris Doner

646pp. Ref. 448-8
Straightforward discussion, abundant examples, and a concise reference guide to graphics commands make this book a must for Windows programmers. Topics range from how Windows works to programming for business, animation, CAD, and desktop publishing. For Version 2.

Hard Disk Instant Reference
SYBEX Prompter Series
Judd Robbins
256pp. Ref. 587-5, 4 ¾" × 8"
Compact yet comprehensive, this pocket-sized reference presents the essential information on DOS commands used in managing directories and files, and in optimizing disk configuration. Includes a survey of third-party utility capabilities. Through DOS 4.0.

The IBM PC-DOS Handbook
(Third Edition)
Richard Allen King
359pp. Ref. 512-3
A guide to the inner workings of PC-DOS 3.2, for intermediate to advanced users and programmers of the IBM PC series. Topics include disk, screen and port control, batch files, networks, compatibility, and more. Through Version 3.3.

Inside DOS: A Programmer's
Guide
Michael J. Young
490pp. Ref. 710-X
A collection of practical techniques (with source code listings) designed to help you take advantage of the rich resources intrinsic to MS-DOS machines. Designed for the experienced programmer with a basic understanding of C and 8086 assembly language, and DOS fundamentals.

Mastering DOS
(Second Edition)
Judd Robbins
722pp. Ref. 555-7
"The most useful DOS book." This seven-part, in-depth tutorial addresses the needs of users at all levels. Topics range from running applications, to managing files and directories, configuring the system, batch file programming, and techniques for system developers. Through Version 4.

MS-DOS Advanced
Programming
Michael J. Young
490pp. Ref. 578-6
Practical techniques for maximizing performance in MS-DOS software by

making best use of system resources. Topics include functions, interrupts, devices, multitasking, memory residency and more, with examples in C and assembler. Through Version 3.3.

MS-DOS Handbook
(Third Edition)
Richard Allen King
362pp. Ref. 492-5
This classic has been fully expanded and revised to include the latest features of MS-DOS Version 3.3. Two reference books in one, this title has separate sections for programmer and user. Multi-DOS partitons, 3 ½-inch disk format, batch file call and return feature, and comprehensive coverage of MS-DOS commands are included. Through Version 3.3.

MS-DOS Power User's Guide,
Volume I
(Second Edition)
Jonathan Kamin
482pp. Ref. 473-9
A fully revised, expanded edition of our best-selling guide to high-performance DOS techniques and utilities—with details on Version 3.3. Configuration, I/O, directory structures, hard disks, RAM disks, batch file programming, the ANSI.SYS device driver, more. Through Version 3.3.

Programmers Guide to
the OS/2 Presentation Manager
Michael J. Young
683pp. Ref. 569-7
This is the definitive tutorial guide to writing programs for the OS/2 Presentation Manager. Young starts with basic architecture, and explores every important feature including scroll bars, keyboard and mouse interface, menus and accelerators, dialogue boxes, clipboards, multitasking, and much more.

Programmer's Guide to
Windows
(Second Edition)
David Durant
Geta Carlson
Paul Yao
704pp. Ref. 496-8
The first edition of this programmer's guide was hailed as a classic. This new edition covers Windows 2 and Windows/386 in depth. Special emphasis is given to over fifty new routines to the Windows interface, and to preparation for OS/2 Presentation Manager compatibility.

Understanding DOS 3.3
Judd Robbins
678pp. Ref. 648-0
This best selling, in-depth tutorial addresses the needs of users at all levels with many examples and hands-on exercises. Robbins discusses the fundamentals of DOS, then covers manipulating files and directories, using the DOS editor, printing, communicating, and finishes with a full section on batch files.

Understanding Hard Disk
Management on the PC
Jonathan Kamin
500pp. Ref. 561-1
This title is a key productivity tool for all hard disk users who want efficient, error-free file management and organization. Includes details on the best ways to conserve hard disk space when using several memory-guzzling programs. Through DOS 4.

Up & Running
with Your Hard Disk
Klaus M Rubsam
140pp. Ref. 666-9
A far-sighted, compact introduction to hard disk installation and basic DOS use. Perfect for PC users who want the practical essentials in the shortest possible time. In 20 basic steps, learn to choose your hard disk, work with accessories, back up data, use DOS utilities to save time, and more.

Up & Running with Windows
286/386
Gabriele Wentges
132pp. Ref. 691-X
This handy 20-step overview gives PC users all the essentials of using Windows - - whether for evaluating the software, or getting a fast start. Each self-contained lesson takes just 15 minutes to one hour to complete.

WORD PROCESSING

The ABC's of Microsoft Word
(Third Edition)
Alan R. Neibauer
461pp. Ref. 604-9
This is for the novice WORD user who wants to begin producing documents in the shortest time possible. Each chapter has short, easy-to-follow lessons for both

keyboard and mouse, including all the basic editing, formatting and printing functions. Version 5.0.

The ABC's of WordPerfect
Alan R. Neibauer
239pp. Ref. 425-9
This basic introduction to WordPefect consists of short, step-by-step lessons—for new users who want to get going fast. Topics range from simple editing and formatting, to merging, sorting, macros, and more. Includes version 4.2

The ABC's of WordPerfect 5
Alan R. Neibauer
283pp. Ref. 504-2
This introduction explains the basics of desktop publishing with WordPerfect 5: editing, layout, formatting, printing, sorting, merging, and more. Readers are shown how to use WordPerfect 5's new features to produce great-looking reports.

The ABC's of WordPerfect 5.1
Alan R. Neibauer
352pp. Ref. 672-3
Neibauer's delightful writing style makes this clear tutorial an especially effective learning tool. Learn all about 5.1's new drop-down menus and mouse capabilities that reduce the tedious memorization of function keys.

Advanced Techniques in Microsoft Word (Second Edition)
Alan R. Neibauer
462pp. Ref. 615-4
This highly acclaimed guide to WORD is an excellent tutorial for intermediate to advanced users. Topics include word processing fundamentals, desktop publishing with graphics, data management, and working in a multiuser environment. For Versions 4 and 5.

Advanced Techniques in MultiMate
Chris Gilbert
275pp. Ref. 412-7
A textbook on efficient use of MultiMate for business applications, in a series of self-contained lessons on such topics as multiple columns, high-speed merging, mailing-list printing and Key Procedures.

Advanced Techniques in WordPerfect 5
Kay Yarborough Nelson
586pp. Ref. 511-5
Now updated for Version 5, this invaluable guide to the advanced features of Word-Perfect provides step-by-step instructions

and practical examples covering those specialized techniques which have most perplexed users—indexing, outlining, foreign-language typing, mathematical functions, and more.

The Complete Guide to MultiMate
Carol Holcomb Dreger
208pp. Ref. 229-9
This step-by-step tutorial is also an excellent reference guide to MultiMate features and uses. Topics include search/replace, library and merge functions, repagination, document defaults and more.

Encyclopedia WordPerfect 5.1
Greg Harvey
Kay Yarborough Nelson
1100pp. Ref. 676-6
This comprehensive, up-to-date Word-Perfect reference is a must for beginning and experienced users alike. With complete, easy-to-find information on every WordPerfect feature and command -- and it's organized by practical functions, with business users in mind.

Introduction to WordStar
Arthur Naiman
208pp. Ref. 134-9
This all time bestseller is an engaging first-time introduction to word processing as well as a complete guide to using WordStar—from basic editing to blocks, global searches, formatting, dot commands, SpellStar and MailMerge. Through Version 3.3.

Mastering DisplayWrite 4
Michael E. McCarthy
447pp. Ref. 510-7
Total training, reference and support for users at all levels—in plain, non-technical language. Novices will be up and running in an hour's time; everyone will gain complete word-processing and document-management skills.

Mastering Microsoft Word on the IBM PC (Fourth Edition)
Matthew Holtz
680pp. Ref. 597-2
This comprehensive, step-by-step guide details all the new desktop publishing developments in this versatile word processor, including details on editing, formatting, printing, and laser printing. Holtz uses sample business documents to demonstrate the use of different fonts, graphics, and complex documents. Includes Fast Track speed notes. For Versions 4 and 5.

Mastering MultiMate Advantage II
Charles Ackerman
407pp. Ref. 482-8
This comprehensive tutorial covers all the capabilities of MultiMate, and highlights the differences between MultiMate Advantage II and previous versions—in pathway support, sorting, math, DOS access, using dBASE III, and more. With many practical examples, and a chapter on the On-File database.

Mastering WordPerfect
Susan Baake Kelly
435pp. Ref. 332-5
Step-by-step training from startup to mastery, featuring practical uses (form letters, newsletters and more), plus advanced topics such as document security and macro creation, sorting and columnar math. Through Version 4.2.

Mastering WordPerfect 5
Susan Baake Kelly
709pp. Ref. 500-X
The revised and expanded version of this definitive guide is now on WordPerfect 5 and covers wordprocessing and basic desktop publishing. As more than 200,000 readers of the original edition can attest, no tutorial approaches it for clarity and depth of treatment. Sorting, line drawing, and laser printing included.

Mastering WordPerfect 5.1
Alan Simpson
1050pp. Ref. 670-7
The ultimate guide for the WordPerfect user. Alan Simpson, the "master communicator," puts you in charge of the latest features of 5.1: new dropdown menus and mouse capabilities, along with the desktop publishing, macro programming, and file conversion functions that have made WordPerfect the most popular word processing program on the market.

Mastering WordStar Release 5.5
Greg Harvey
David J. Clark
450pp. Ref. 491-7
This book is the ultimate reference book for the newest version of WordStar. Readers may use Mastering to look up any word processing function, including the new Version 5 and 5.5 features and enhancements, and find detailed instructions for fundamental to advanced operations.

Microsoft Word Instant Reference for the IBM PC
Matthew Holtz
266pp. Ref. 692-8

Turn here for fast, easy access to concise information on every command and feature of Microsoft Word version 5.0 -- for editing, formatting, merging, style sheets, macros, and more. With exact keystroke sequences, discussion of command options, and commonly-performed tasks.

Practical WordStar Uses
Julie Anne Arca
303pp. Ref. 107-1
A hands-on guide to WordStar and MailMerge applications, with solutions to comon problems and "recipes" for day-to-day tasks. Formatting, merge-printing and much more; plus a quick-reference command chart and notes on CP/M and PC-DOS. For Version 3.3.

Understanding Professional Write
Gerry Litton
400pp. Ref. 656-1
A complete guide to Professional Write that takes you from creating your first simple document, into a detailed description of all major aspects of the software. Special features place an emphasis on the use of different typestyles to create attractive documents as well as potential problems and suggestions on how to get around them.

Understanding WordStar 2000
David Kolodney
Thomas Blackadar
275pp. Ref. 554-9
This engaging, fast-paced series of tutorials covers everything from moving the cursor to print enhancements, format files, key glossaries, windows and MailMerge. With practical examples, and notes for former WordStar users.

Visual Guide to WordPerfect
Jeff Woodward
457pp. Ref. 591-3
This is a visual hands-on guide which is ideal for brand new users as the book shows each activity keystroke-by-keystroke. Clear illustrations of computer screen menus are included at every stage. Covers basic editing, formatting lines, paragraphs, and pages, using the block feature, footnotes, search and replace, and more. Through Version 5.

WordPerfect 5 Desktop Companion
SYBEX Ready Reference Series
Greg Harvey
Kay Yarborough Nelson
1006pp. Ref. 522-0

Desktop publishing features have been added to this compact encyclopedia. This title offers more detailed, cross-referenced entries on every software features including page formatting and layout, laser printing and word processing macros. New users of WordPerfect, and those new to Version 5 and desktop publishing will find this easy to use for on-the-job help.

WordPerfect Instant Reference
SYBEX Prompter Series
Greg Harvey
Kay Yarborough Nelson
254pp. Ref. 476-3, 4 ¾" × 8"
When you don't have time to go digging through the manuals, this fingertip guide offers clear, concise answers: command summaries, correct usage, and exact keystroke sequences for on-the-job tasks. Convenient organization reflects the structure of WordPerfect. Through Version 4.2.

WordPerfect 5 Instant Reference
SYBEX Prompter Series
Greg Harvey
Kay Yarborough Nelson
316pp. Ref. 535-2, 4 ¾" × 8"
This pocket-sized reference has all the program commands for the powerful WordPerfect 5 organized alphabetically for quick access. Each command entry has the exact key sequence, any reveal codes, a list of available options, and option-by-option discussions.

WordPerfect 5.1 Instant Reference
Greg Harvey
Kay Yarborough Nelson
252pp. Ref. 674-X

WordPerfect 5 Macro Handbook
Kay Yarborough Nelson
488pp. Ref. 483-6
Readers can create macros customtailored to their own needs with this excellent tutorial and reference. Nelson's expertise guides the WordPerfect 5 user through nested and chained macros, macro libraries, specialized macros, and much more.

WordPerfect 5.1 Tips and Tricks (Fourth Edition)
Alan R. Neibauer
675pp. Ref. 681-2
This new edition is a real timesaver. For on-the-job guidance and creative new uses, this title covers all versions of WordPerfect up to and including 5.1—streamlining documents, automating with macros, new print enhancements, and more.

WordStar Instant Reference
SYBEX Prompter Series
David J. Clark
314pp. Ref. 543-3, 4 ¾" × 8"
This quick reference provides reminders on the use of the editing, formatting, mailmerge, and document processing commands available through WordStar 4 and 5. Operations are organized alphabetically for easy access. The text includes a survey of the menu system and instructions for installing and customizing WordStar.

SYBEX Computer Books are different.

Here is why . . .

At SYBEX, each book is designed with you in mind. Every manuscript is carefully selected and supervised by our editors, who are themselves computer experts. We publish the best authors, whose technical expertise is matched by an ability to write clearly and to communicate effectively. Programs are thoroughly tested for accuracy by our technical staff. Our computerized production department goes to great lengths to make sure that each book is well-designed.

In the pursuit of timeliness, SYBEX has achieved many publishing firsts. SYBEX was among the first to integrate personal computers used by authors and staff into the publishing process. SYBEX was the first to publish books on the CP/M operating system, microprocessor interfacing techniques, word processing, and many more topics.

Expertise in computers and dedication to the highest quality product have made SYBEX a world leader in computer book publishing. Translated into fourteen languages, SYBEX books have helped millions of people around the world to get the most from their computers. We hope we have helped you, too.

For a complete catalog of our publications:

SYBEX, Inc. 2021 Challenger Drive, #100, Alameda, CA 94501
Tel: (415) 523-8233/(800) 227-2346 Telex: 336311
Fax: (415) 523-2373